The
FEAST OF
FICTION
Kitchen

The FEAST OF FICTION *Kitchen*

RECIPES INSPIRED BY TV, MOVIES, GAMES & BOOKS

JIMMY WONG & ASHLEY ADAMS

THE COUNTRYMAN PRESS

A division of W. W. Norton & Company

Independent Publisher Since 1923

Copyright © 2020 by Jimmy Wong

All rights reserved
Printed in China

For information about permission to
reproduce selections from this book, write
to Permissions, The Countryman Press,
500 Fifth Avenue, New York, NY 10110

For information about special discounts for
bulk purchases, please contact W. W. Norton
Special Sales at specialsales@wwnorton.com
or 800-233-4830

Manufacturing by RR Donnelley, Shenzhen
Book design by Paul Nielsen, Faceout Studio
Production manager: Devon Zahn

The Countryman Press
www.countrymanpress.com

A division of W. W. Norton & Company, Inc.
500 Fifth Avenue, New York, NY 10110
www.wwnorton.com

978-1-68268-440-5

10 9 8 7 6 5 4 3 2 1

This book is dedicated to every grown-up
who is still a kid at heart.

Contents

Baking Essentials   *173*

Introduction

"Hey Ashley, what do you know about fondant?"

It was a chilly day at Disneyland (okay, it was 60 degrees—but to be fair, that is practically frigid by Los Angeles standards), and the *Feast of Fiction* cooking show was but a twinkle in Jimmy's eye. Though we were supposed to be celebrating a mutual friend's birthday, the rides and churros faded into the background as we realized the kind of magic we could be making. Between Jimmy's videomaking experience and Ashley's love—and, let's face it, far superior knowledge—of baking, *Feast of Fiction* came to life.

We envisioned a cooking show that was one part recipes and five parts nostalgia. Our childhood experiences and grown-up imaginations fueled every writing session, every late-night edit. We understood that you can own a food processor and still love *SpongeBob SquarePants*, that you can appreciate a fancy wine pairing with a *Game of Thrones*–themed dessert. And you can certainly enjoy a day at Disneyland but still be a BOSS at fondant.

Since that first conversation nine years ago, we've celebrated over 300 *Feast of Fiction* videos. Over 180 million people across the globe have tuned in—WHAT?! 180 *million*?! That's jaw-dropping. Together, we've seen so many movies, shows, and games that have come and gone: *Game of Thrones, Minecraft, Breaking Bad, Mulan, Star Wars, Star Trek, Harry Potter, Steven Universe* . . . the list goes on! One of the best parts about creating our show is that we can continue to fan over our old staples while looking forward to whatever is coming out next.

We wish our little kitchen could fit all of you, but this book might be the next best thing. It's our way of feasting together, and, more than anything, our way of saying thank you. Thank you for sharing your favorite fictional foods with us, and for your comments, and for your unbelievable support.

Here are some of our best recipes fine-tuned and improved for use in kitchens everywhere. We hope you love them as much as we do.

See you in the Fiction Kitchen!

Jimmy & Ashley

BLACK PEPPER

CAYENNE

CHILI POWDER

CINNAMON

CUMIN

FENNEL

GARLIC POWDER

GARLIC SALT

GINGER

ITALIAN
SEASONING

MARJORAM

NUTMEG

NOTES ON INGREDIENTS

We know that the kitchen can be a daunting place, especially when you're making foods from all of these different worlds and universes. We've taken extra care to make sure our recipes are as accessible as possible to everyday cooks, bakers, and aspiring chefs. We get it—sometimes you just can't make *every* single thing from scratch. Throughout this cookbook, you'll find reference recipes for basic baking foundations, cheat codes on ways to make your life a little easier, and tips and tricks for everyone on the cooking spectrum.

When it comes to food and drink in movies, TV shows, and cartoons, it has a tendency to be all sorts of cool colors. It was important to us to use natural forms of food coloring in as many recipes as we could, as long as it didn't compromise the core aesthetic of the recipe. Several recipes of ours use butterfly pea powder for a natural blue food dye. You might have to take a trip to a specialty grocery store to find it, as well as any of our other unique and specific tools or ingredients.

Finally, we have an assortment of drink recipes, some of which are alcoholic. If you would rather not have any alcohol in your drink, you can simply remove it from the recipe and then you have turned it into a delicious and non-alcoholic mocktail! Easy as that.

GLOSSARY OF COOKING TERMS

Bain-marie: Essentially a "hot water bath," this is a good way to cook cheesecakes or custard-based cakes by incorporating water or steam to ensure a more even cooking process.

Beat: To mix rapidly in order to make a mixture smooth and light by incorporating as much air as possible.

Blend: To incorporate two or more ingredients thoroughly.

Bloom: The process of softening gelatin sheets in liquid prior to using in a recipe.

Boil: To heat a liquid in a pot until bubbles break continually on the surface.

Cream: To soften butter by beating it at room temperature. Butter and sugar are often creamed together until light and fluffy.

Dice: To cut food into small cubes of uniform size and shape.

Dock: Piercing the bottom of a piecrust in order to release air, helping to eliminate air bubbles in the crust.

Fold: To fold your ingredients together, dip a spoon through the center of your mixture, turn it to scoop upward, and bring the contents to the top. Repeat this process while slowly rotating the bowl, until the ingredients are thoroughly combined.

Ganache: A glaze, icing, or filling created by combining equal parts chocolate and cream. There are different variations of ganache based on different types of chocolate and their cocoa butter-to-sugar ratio.

Grate: To create tiny shreds of food using a grater.

Knead: To work and press dough with the palms of the hands or mechanically, to develop the gluten in the flour.

Mince: To cut or chop food into extremely small pieces.

Pâte brisée: The French term for piecrust pastry.

Pâte sucrée: The French term for a pastry that is sweeter than a typical piecrust. It's most often used for tarts.

Pinch: A pinch is typically the amount of salt, pepper, or dried herb that you can hold between your thumb and forefinger.

Poach: A cooking technique where food is submerged in liquid and cooked using low temperatures.

Proof: A process in breadmaking that allows the "final rise" of the dough before baking by letting the dough rest in a warm environment.

Puree: Mashing foods until perfectly smooth, usually by using a blender or food processor.

Steam: A method of cooking food in a steamer pot, using the boiling water underneath to create hot steam.

Stiff peaks: Firm tips of whipped cream or egg whites that can usually stand on their own. You can test to see if you have stiff peaks by flipping over the mixing bowl to see if the peaks stay put.

Swiss meringue buttercream: A buttercream frosting in which you create a meringue from egg whites and granulated sugar, as opposed to an American buttercream created with powdered sugar.

Temper: A term used for integrating eggs into a hot mixture without scrambling the eggs.

Whip: The process of beating an ingredient vigorously to incorporate air.

EQUIPMENT

Cooking with the right equipment can make life in the kitchen so much easier and more fun. We've been making the Feast of Fiction videos for nearly a decade, and the assortment of tools and gadgets that have passed through our set is far too vast to count. That being said, acquiring the right equipment should be more about quality than quantity. Here is a list of the kitchen tools and equipment that will be crucial to making the recipes in this book, as well as everything you need to make your kitchen hum.

Good cutting boards: A solid and reliable cutting board will make prepping ingredients much more simple and efficient. We recommend a heavier wooden cutting board for veggies and cooked food, while a separate plastic cutting board is ideal for raw meats or fish to avoid cross-contamination.

A solid set of pots and pans: You really only need a saucepan and skillet to cook almost anything in the kitchen. Stainless steel cookware is preferable, but you can make do with any ol' saucepan, skillet, stockpot, and so on.

A durable set of knives: Many chefs will argue that the knife is the single most important tool in the kitchen, and it's hard to disagree. If you buy a good knife today and take care of it, you could be using it for the rest of your life! A set of knives should include a chef's knife, paring knife, utility knife, and bread knife, which will cover you in almost every knife scenario.

Mixing bowls: Cooking needs a lot of preparation, and mixing bowls are incredibly helpful when cooking with many different ingredients. Stainless steel or glass are preferred, and trust us when we say you'll find tons of other uses for these mixing bowls in the future.

Measuring cups and spoons: Whether you're baking or cooking on a stovetop, you'll always be measuring ingredients. You should have a set of both dry and wet measuring cups.

Stand mixer or hand mixer: If you'd like to be a hero and knead or mix your ingredients by hand, go right ahead. If you'd like to save time and not break a sweat every time you bake, we highly recommend having a stand mixer or hand mixer. You'll be kneading dough, whipping cream, mixing batter, beating frosting, and more—make your life easier with a mixer.

Blender, food processor, or immersion blender: This will help make purees, soups, and smoothies.

Baking sheets and cake pans: There are a few different types of baking sheets and cake pans to invest in when creating these recipes. It's essential to have a standard cookie sheet in your baking arsenal. Also, an 8- or 9-inch round cake pan is always good to have lying around for building cakes, as well as a metal or silicone muffin tin for creating cupcakes. We use some specialty pans for certain recipes, which you can find at most grocery stores.

A set of round cookie or biscuit cutters: We use a round cookie cutter throughout the book, and collecting a set of them will give you more size options for your recipe. You can also use a circular object like a bowl or glass to hand trace the shape.

Assorted gel food coloring: Affordable options can be found at your local craft stores or online retailers.

Parchment paper: Many of our recipes make use of parchment paper. Lining your cake pans with parchment paper is an absolute necessity, as it makes removing cakes a lot easier and also reduces the risk of the cake splitting. It can also be used for handy DIY homemade stencils by tracing the desired design on the paper and cutting it out with kitchen shears. This will be necessary for cutting out the required design in pastry needed for specific recipes in this book.

Other equipment that isn't necessary, but good to have on hand:

Candy thermometer: A cooking thermometer that can accurately measure high temperatures in liquid solutions; also useful for deep frying.

Cooling rack: For cooling cakes, cookies, and any other baked goods coming out of the oven.

Kitchen shears: Strong scissors specifically for the kitchen, used to cut ingredients, stencils, and so on.

Lemon press: For freshly squeezed lemon juice.

Mandolin slicer: For creating thin and consistent slices of fruits and vegetables.

Microplane grater: For zesting fruit and fine grating.

Pastry cutter: For mixing and mashing ingredients, like butter into dry goods while baking.

Plastic bench scraper: An inexpensive plastic tool used for specialty cakes, helping to smooth the frosting for a cleaner and more professional appearance.

Breakfast

BREAKFAST CONGEE

(Inspired by *Mulan*)

Getting down to business to defeat a deadly invading force is no easy task, and as we all know, breakfast is the most important meal of the day. That's why it's important to start things off with a smile, and a delicious recipe to boot. This congee is filling, hearty, and topped with two fried eggs and a big slice of bacon. A perfect mix of Western and Chinese culture, this breakfast porridge will prepare you for the battles of everyday life. No lucky cricket necessary!

Prep Time: 45 minutes
Total Time: 1 hour
Serves: 1 Man, swift as the coursing river, or 1 Girl worth fighting for

Ingredients

¼ cup rice

½ teaspoon cooking oil

1 slice bacon

2 large eggs

Instructions

1 Add the rice and 4 cups of water to a medium saucepan. Bring to a boil over medium heat, keeping the lid open until the congee becomes thick, like a soup consistency, and the rice disappears into the water, 30 to 45 minutes.

2 Fry the bacon in a frying pan, but don't let it get too crispy. The bacon slice should still be able to be curved or shaped. Place the bacon on a paper towel–lined plate in a U-shape to create the bacon smile.

3 In the same frying pan over medium-low heat, add the cooking oil and the eggs, cooking until over easy.

4 In a medium bowl, add the congee and place the eggs for the eyes and the bacon for the smile.

HOT BUTTERED SCONES

(Inspired by *The Hobbit*)

J.R.R. Tolkien once said a scone goes great with a huge jug of coffee. So grab your favorite jug and get ready to add these to your breakfast spread. These are perfect for breakfast, either first or second, elevenses, or even afternoon tea. This recipe is inspired by a classic scone recipe—a perfect blend of savory and sweet. Flaky and buttery, with a pop of sweetness from the turbinado sugar that finishes the top, it's the perfect bite: soft with a little crunch.

Prep Time: 10 minutes
Total Time: 30 minutes
Serves: 8 breakfasting Halflings

Ingredients

2 cups all-purpose flour

¼ cup granulated sugar

½ teaspoon kosher salt

½ teaspoon baking soda

1 tablespoon baking powder

8 tablespoons (1 stick) unsalted butter, softened and cubed, plus 1 tablespoon for brushing, melted

1 large egg

⅔ cup buttermilk

½ teaspoon vanilla extract

Turbinado sugar for sprinkling

Instructions

1 Preheat the oven to 400°F. Line a baking sheet with parchment paper.

2 Mix the flour, sugar, salt, baking soda, and baking powder in a large bowl.

3 Mix in the ½ cup softened (but not melted) butter with a fork or a pastry cutter until the dough resembles pea-sized crumbs.

4 In a separate bowl, whisk together the egg, buttermilk, and vanilla to combine.

5 Create a well in the flour mixture and pour the wet ingredients into the dry ingredients and work together until a crumbly dough forms.

6 Drop the dough onto a floured surface and knead a couple of times into a ball. Roll out the dough into a circle about an inch thick.

7 Cut out eight scones as if you are slicing a pizza. Place the slices on the prepared baking sheet, brush with the melted butter, and sprinkle with turbinado sugar. Bake for 20 to 22 minutes until golden brown.

FIRE SALT DONUTS

(Inspired by *Steven Universe*)

While the results aren't going to be breathing fire, eating this donut will certainly test your taste buds in a way no donut ever has. Steven Universe has a long history of making all sorts of crazy foods in the show, and this donut fits right into the pantheon of epic foods we've been dying to interpret. So give it a taste if you dare—you'll be screaming for ice cream in no time with this fiery confection.

Prep Time: 5 minutes
Total Time: 30 minutes
Serves: 6 joking victims

Ingredients

1 cup plus 1 teaspoon all-purpose flour

1 teaspoon baking powder

⅓ cup granulated sugar

½ teaspoon nutmeg

½ teaspoon ghost pepper sea salt, plus more for sprinkling

2 tablespoons unsalted butter

¼ cup whole milk, warm

¼ cup plain yogurt

1 teaspoon vanilla extract

1 large egg, beaten

Strawberry Pop Rocks

Glaze

1 cup white chocolate chips

¼ cup heavy cream

1 teaspoon corn syrup

1 teaspoon Crystal Hot sauce (or any vinegar-based hot sauce)

Pinch of cayenne

Pinch of cinnamon

Red food coloring

Instructions

1 Preheat the oven to 350°F. Lightly grease a doughnut pan and line a tray with parchment paper.

2 Sift the flour and baking powder together into a large bowl. Whisk in the sugar, nutmeg, and salt. Add the butter and use your fingers or a fork to mix into the dry ingredients as you would in making a pastry crust, until evenly distributed. Add the warm milk, yogurt, vanilla, and egg and stir until just combined. Do not overmix.

3 Use a piping bag or a spoon to fill the doughnut pan cavities three-fourths of the way full. Bake until the doughnuts are a light golden brown and spring back when touched, about 10 minutes. Let cool slightly before glazing.

4 While doughnuts are cooling, prepare the glaze. In a microwave safe bowl, combine the white chocolate chips, heavy cream, and corn syrup. Heat for 45 seconds in the microwave. Remove, give it a stir, and let sit for a couple of minutes for the residual chips to melt. Stir in the hot sauce, cayenne, cinnamon, and just a small dab of red food coloring.

5 Dip the donuts into the glaze. Place on the parchment paper–lined tray. Sprinkle with ghost pepper sea salt to taste and pop rocks before the glaze sets.

CACTUS JUICE

(Inspired by *Avatar: The Last Airbender*)

We're not going to beat around the proverbial bush—or cactus—when it comes to this cactus juice. It'll quench ya. Nothing's quenchier! It's the darndest quenchiest thing we've ever made, and we hope you'll agree. We can't guarantee it'll have the same mind-bending effects as the version Sokka drank in Avatar: The Last Airbender, *but all things considered, that might be for the best. After all, we're ultimately just after the quenchiest drink we can make.*

Prep Time: 10 minutes
Total Time: 10 minutes
Makes: 1 cocktail

Ingredients

1 mini watermelon

1 cup frozen pineapple chunks

1½ ounces white rum

One 14-ounce can coconut milk

2 tablespoons lime juice

Instructions

1 Cut a circle out of the top of the watermelon and scoop out the watermelon pulp with a spoon. Set the watermelon shell aside.

2 Place the watermelon pulp in a blender with the pineapple, rum, coconut milk, and lime juice. Blend until smooth.

3 Pour the mixture into the watermelon shell and serve with a bamboo straw (see photo on pages 28–29).

HOME-BREWED SUPER PORP

(Inspired by *Adventure Time*)

Finn and Jake definitely love their grape soda (and spreading the good word), so we took this drink and spiced it up—this cocktail is an alcoholic grape soda. It's fruity, fresh, and a vibrant color thanks to butterfly pea powder and a squeeze of lemon (see photo on pages 32-33). Perform an amazing party trick: Add even just one drop of lemon juice and, oh my glob, the cocktail transforms from blue to a Lumpy Space Princess purple before your eyes!

Prep Time: 10 minutes
Total Time: 15 minutes
Makes: 1 cocktail

Ingredients

1½ ounces Pavan Liqueur

½ ounce freshly squeezed lemon juice

¾ ounce Butterfly Pea Simple Syrup (see page 174)

¾ ounce pasteurized egg whites

Splash of lemon lime soda

Instructions

1 Add the Pavan, lemon juice, Butterfly Pea Simple Syrup, and egg whites to a cocktail shaker. Add ice and shake vigorously for 15 seconds, making sure the egg white becomes frothy.

2 Pour over ice into a Collins glass or tumbler, and top with a splash of lemon lime soda.

MILK OF THE POPPY

(Inspired by *Game of Thrones*)

In *Game of Thrones, milk of the poppy* is basically the standard cure-all of the Seven Kingdoms—the elite use it as a sleep aid, painkiller, and anxiety reducer. Oh, and if taken in excess amounts, it can poison your enemies. But, as much as we respect the Maesters of the Citadel, we think that might be a bit extreme for our needs. So we've concocted this whiskey-based elixir that His Grace, King Robert, would approve. We've added Drambuie, a botanical spirit sweetened with honey, which was known in olden times to have medicinal purposes. Sure, it's a stretch, but at least none of your favorite characters had to die in the making of this recipe!

Prep Time: 1 hour 15 minutes
Total Time: 1 hour 15 minutes
Makes: 2 to 3 cocktails

Ingredients

¼ cup poppy seeds

3 tablespoons honey

1 ounce Jameson Irish Whiskey

½ ounce Drambuie

¾ ounce Frangelico

Instructions

1 In a small saucepan, add the poppy seeds, honey, and 1½ cups of water. Bring to a rolling boil. Remove from the heat and let sit for 1 hour.

2 Pour the poppy mixture into a blender, and process until smooth. Strain the mixture through a cheesecloth or fine mesh sieve and set aside.

3 In a mixing glass or small pitcher, combine the whiskey, Drambuie, and Frangelico. Add the poppy mixture and stir well. Serve in a chilled martini glass or as a chilled shot.

BANTHA BLUE MILK

(Inspired by Star Wars)

Do you think the people who decided to color the milk blue in Star Wars would ever have predicted that it would become a pop culture icon, decades after the movie's original release? Instead of traveling to Tatooine to milk a giant, furry space buffalo, we used The Force to create this simple banana smoothie recipe. It gets its blue hue from natural food color and is way more flavorful than boring Earth milk. Yummy and healthy it is, young Jedi!

Prep Time: 5 minutes
Total Time: 5 minutes
Serves: 2 cantina band players

Ingredients

1 cup milk

1 ripe banana

2 tablespoons Greek yogurt

1 tablespoon honey

½ teaspoon butterfly pea powder

½ cup ice

Instructions

1 Add the milk, banana, yogurt, and honey to a blender and process until smooth, about 15 seconds.

2 Add the butterfly pea powder and ice. Continue to blend until the ice is incorporated and the blue color mixes in throughout the drink.

3 Serve in a tumbler.

HEART POTION SANGRIA

(Inspired by *The Legend of Zelda*)

Hey, listen. Heart potions feature in nearly every Zelda game, and a good sangria is a staple of any summer party. Inspired by an Aperol spritz, we infused this sangria with the very appropriate blood orange and other red fruits. Whether you need a pick-me-up in the middle of your adventures in Hyrule, or a rest from all the battling, this sangria is here to keep you going!

Prep Time: 15 minutes
Total Time: 4 hours 15 minutes
Serves: 6 to 8 Hylian heroes

Ingredients

One 750-ml bottle Sauvignon Blanc
¼ cup Aperol
1 cup club soda
1 apple, thinly sliced
1 cup sliced strawberries
1 cup raspberries
Freshly squeezed juice of 6 blood oranges

Instructions

1 Combine the wine, Aperol, club soda, apple, strawberries, raspberries, and blood orange juice in a large pitcher or drink receptacle.

2 Stir well and let it sit in the fridge for at least 4 hours before serving.

KELP SHAKE

(Inspired by *SpongeBob SquarePants*)

The real question when making a drink inspired by SpongeBob SquarePants is how exactly do the citizens of Bikini Bottom actually drink anything if they're already underwater? Wouldn't it just, like, float to the surface? Cups would be completely useless . . . right? RIGHT?! Logic aside, this dairy-free green smoothie is rich in nutrients and flavor, and some kelp extract gives it that essence of the ocean and Plankton green color.

Prep Time: 5 minutes
Total Time: 5 minutes
Serves: 1 passionate fry cook

Ingredients

3 cups coconut water

2 cups frozen pineapple chunks

1 cup kale

1 cup spinach

½ cup chopped green apple

1 ripe banana

Freshly squeezed juice of 1 lemon

1 tablespoon honey

1 teaspoon kelp extract or powder

1 cup ice

Instructions

1 Add all of the ingredients to a blender and process until smooth and uniformly green. Serve and enjoy, mateys!

ROMULAN ALE

They say Romulan Ale is the strongest alcohol in the universe—and while that prospect is entertaining, we also realize it's thoroughly impractical. And dangerous. How are you supposed to pilot the Enterprise home? You'd have to call a space taxi. How much would a ride to the Alpha Quadrant cost anyway? Besides, real Romulan Ale is technically illegal in Federation territory. So, instead, we've got a blue Romulan Ale that's inspired by a classic cocktail—and we're using natural butterfly pea powder as opposed to your typical blue Curaçao. So bottoms up, and may you boldly drink where no man has drunk before!

Total Time: 5 minutes
Serves: 2 off-duty Starfleet officers

Ingredients

2 ounces vodka or gin
½ ounce Butterfly Pea Simple Syrup (see page 174)
Equal parts soda water and Sprite

Instructions

1 In a cocktail shaker, add the vodka or gin and the Butterfly Pea Simple Syrup with ice and shake.

2 Fill a highball glass with ice. Strain the contents of the shaker into the glass. Top with equal parts soda water and Sprite and serve.

NECTAR SMOOTHIE

(Inspired by the Percy Jackson series)

This is what Zeus drinks for breakfast. This nutritious smoothie is as close to the Nectar of the Gods as we mortals are going to get. Using protein-rich Greek yogurt and raw honey, with protein-packed chia seeds and goji berries for additional energy, this is basically a healthy version of an ambrosia salad in smoothie form.

Prep Time: 10 minutes
Total Time: 10 minutes
Serves: 2 Half-Blood campers

Ingredients

1 cup fresh pineapple chunks

½ orange, peeled

1 ripe banana, peeled

1 tablespoon chia seeds

⅓ cup dried goji berries

¼ cup shredded coconut

1 cup Greek yogurt

½ cup milk (any type)

2 tablespoons raw honey

1 cup ice

Instructions

1 Put the pineapple, orange, banana, chia seeds, goji berries, and coconut in a blender. Add the yogurt, milk, honey, and ice. Blend until smooth.

HOME-BREWED BUTTERBEER

(Inspired by the Harry Potter series)

Butterbeer might be one of the most well-known aspects of the Harry Potter universe. It made our mouths water the first time we read about it in the books, and seeing Harry and his friends enjoy it at the Hogsmeade Tavern in the movies was more than enough for us to know we just had to make this recipe come to life. Delicious, sweet, and the perfect amount of refreshing, this recipe is our ode to one of the greatest fantasy series of all time. Next fantasy? Getting that invite by owl to attend Hogwarts. We can dream, right?

Prep Time: 15 minutes
Total Time: 18 minutes
Serves: 1 or 2 Hogwarts students

Ingredients

Butterscotch Sauce

4 tablespoons salted butter

1 cup packed dark brown sugar

3/4 cup heavy cream

Pinch of salt

1 tablespoon vanilla extract

Beer

1 tablespoon unsalted butter

1/2 cup Butterscotch Sauce, plus more for drizzling

One 12-ounce bottle cream soda

Whipped cream, for topping

Instructions

❶ To make the Butterscotch Sauce: Melt the salted butter in a medium saucepan on low-medium heat. Add the brown sugar, heavy cream, and salt and stir with a wooden spoon or spatula until well combined. Cook for 7 to 9 minutes or until the mixture reaches 225°F on a candy thermometer, stirring frequently to prevent burning. Remove from heat and stir in the vanilla extract. Once cooled, transfer to an airtight container.

❷ To make the Beer: In a small heatproof bowl, melt the unsalted butter in the microwave. Add 1/2 cup of the Butterscotch Sauce and mix well.

❸ Pour the cream soda into a frozen mug, add the butter-Butterscotch Sauce mixture, and whisk together.

❹ Top with the whipped cream and drizzle with extra Butterscotch Sauce.

⚡ *Cheat Code:* A variation can be made to this drink by heating the cream soda in the microwave for 30 seconds, and then adding the warm butter-Butterscotch Sauce mixture to it.

Appetizers & Sides

SAVORY PUMPKIN PASTIES

(inspired by the Harry Potter series)

Accio *delicious food! Wands up if you ever read Harry Potter and drooled over the vivid descriptions of all the wondrous food and delights that abound in the wizarding world.* ***all wands go up*** *This is our way of turning our own kitchen into the Honeydukes cart on the Hogwarts Express. BECAUSE WE ARE GROWN-UPS. Pasties are traditionally made with meat and vegetables in the United Kingdom, so we decided to create a savory take on the pumpkin pasty. Serve to fellow Ravenclaws as an appetizer or make it a magical main course. Either way, you'll be nominated as Head Boy or Girl faster than you can say, "Nimbus 2000."*

Prep Time: 2 hours 50 minutes
Total Time: 3 hours 10 minutes
Serves: 20 Muggles

Ingredients

½ cup chopped onion

3 baby bella mushrooms

2 celery stalks

½ cup sweet potato

½ cup carrot

½ cup cauliflower

4 tablespoons olive oil

4 garlic cloves

½ teaspoon fresh thyme

1 teaspoon fresh rosemary

8 ounces pumpkin puree

¼ cup canned coconut milk

¼ cup vegetable broth

½ teaspoon nutmeg

Salt

Freshly ground black pepper

1 recipe Piecrust (see page 175) or 1 frozen or refrigerated ready-made piecrust

1 large egg, for egg wash

Instructions

1. Preheat the oven to 400°F.

2. Mince the onion, mushrooms, celery, sweet potato, carrot, and cauliflower (or pulse a couple of times in a food processor). Toss in 3 tablespoons of the olive oil and set aside. Mince the garlic. Chop the thyme and rosemary.

3. Sauté the garlic, thyme, and rosemary with the remaining 1 tablespoon olive oil in a large skillet on medium heat. Add the minced vegetables and cook until vegetables are translucent, 5 to 7 minutes

4. Reduce the heat to low and add the pumpkin puree, coconut milk, and vegetable broth. Stir. Mix in the nutmeg and salt and pepper to taste. Stir to combine very well.

5. Roll out the piecrust to ⅛ inch thick on a floured surface and cut 20 circles out of your piecrust using either a bowl as a stencil or a 4-inch circle cookie cutter.

continued

6 Place 1 tablespoon of the pumpkin filling on half of one of the circles, making sure it's not too close to the edge. Egg wash the edge and fold the other side onto it. Crimp with a fork to seal the edges. With a sharp knife, cut a lightning bolt (like Harry's scar) into the top of the crust. Brush once more with the egg wash. Repeat for the remaining pasties.

7 Bake for 20 minutes until golden brown.

"Anything from the trolley, dears?"

—Trolley lady

SHRIMP COCKTAIL

(Inspired by *Beetlejuice*)

We grew up watching Tim Burton movies, and this scene in particular stood out to both of us as one that was an absolute delight to watch as we reveled in the terror it elicited from its guests. Shrimp cocktails have never looked so frightening, and the statement this one makes is second to none. It took several kitchen professionals many minutes to get this creeptastic limb to stand upright, so we'd recommend presenting this recipe on a bed of lettuce, for everyone's sake. Please note that you will need a clean plastic glove for constructing this dish.

Prep Time: 1 hour
Total Time: 6 hours 30 minutes
Serves: 2 to 3 mischievous ghouls

Ingredients

2 pounds fresh or frozen uncooked shrimp, peeled and deveined
10 sheets platinum-grade gelatin

Cocktail Sauce
1½ cups ketchup
Zest and freshly squeezed juice of 1 lemon
2 teaspoons powdered horseradish
½ teaspoon Worcestershire sauce
½ teaspoon hot sauce
½ tablespoon garlic salt
¼ teaspoon paprika
⅛ teaspoon cayenne pepper

Instructions

1 Fill a large stockpot with water and bring to a rapid boil. Take off the heat and let the boil subside. Add the shrimp, cover with lid, and let steep for about 5 minutes. Submerge the cooked shrimp into a bowl of ice water to cool.

2 Setting aside 5 shrimp tails, chop shrimp into small pieces.

3 Prepare the Cocktail Sauce by combining all the ingredients in a small bowl. Set aside.

4 Pour 4 cups cold water into a large bowl and add leaves of platinum-grade gelatin to bloom for 5 to 10 minutes. When the gelatin is soft, wring out the water and put the gelatin into a medium saucepan with ½ cup of water over medium heat.

5 Add 1 cup of the cocktail sauce, garlic salt, paprika, and cayenne. Stir until the gelatin is dissolved. Take off the heat and let cool for 10 minutes. Add the chopped shrimp to the saucepan and make sure all the shrimp pieces are coated.

continued

6 Start filling the glove with the chopped shrimp. Pack the shrimp into each of the fingers in the glove, spooning in a little gelatin mixture as you go to ensure stability. Fill the rest of the glove up with chopped shrimp, making sure the glove is packed tightly. Tie the end of the glove with string or a rubber band, and place the hand in a loaf pan to set with a slight, natural looking bend in the fingers. Refrigerate for 5 to 6 hours or until set.

7 Once set, remove the glove from the shrimp hand by using sharp kitchen shears or a utility knife, snipping the string or rubber band off and slowly peeling away the glove from the bottom up. Carefully cut the glove off of each finger. Trim the bottom of the shrimp hand with a sharp knife to create an even surface for the hand to stand upright.

8 When ready to serve, pour rest of the cocktail sauce in the bottom of a shallow bowl. Stand shrimp hand upright in the middle of the bowl. Add tails to the tips of the fingers before serving for aesthetic purposes.

LEMBAS BREAD FOCACCIA

(Inspired by *The Lord of the Rings*)

Just one bite of this Elven bread is said to fill up your stomach for an entire day's journey—but we're pretty sure those rules only apply to citizens of Middle Earth. Our take on lembas bread has more realistic magical qualities: the high olive oil content prevents leftovers from going stale (as long as it's wrapped up in a sealed zipper bag). So bake enough for the Merrys and Pippins in your life, and save some for later, my precious. And don't forget to indent the focaccia dough with that classic lembas bread "X"!

Prep Time: 1 hour 20 minutes
Total Time: 1 hour 45 minutes
Serves: Fills the stomachs of 6 Elves (or 1 Pippin)

Ingredients

2¼ teaspoons (1 envelope) active dry yeast

2 teaspoons granulated sugar

2 cups all-purpose flour

1 teaspoon sea salt, plus 1 additional teaspoon for topping (optional)

¼ cup olive oil, plus more for greasing

Homemade Herbes de Provence

1 teaspoon dried thyme

½ teaspoon dried oregano

¼ teaspoon dried rosemary

¼ teaspoon dried marjoram

½ teaspoon dried parsley

Instructions

1 Prepare a 9-by-13-inch baking pan with olive oil. Set aside.

2 In a small bowl, combine the yeast and sugar with 1 cup warm water and let sit for 15 minutes, or until frothy.

3 To make the Homemade Herbes de Provence, combine all of the herbs into a small bowl and stir to combine.

4 Add the flour, 1 teaspoon of the salt, 2 tablespoons of the olive oil, and Herbes de Provence mixture to the bowl of a stand mixer. Using the dough hook attachment, mix the ingredients on low while slowly adding the yeast mixture. Increase the speed to medium and let the dough turn for 5 more minutes, making sure the dough is fully incorporated. Feel free to add more flour in increments if the dough seems too sticky.

5 Grease a large bowl and transfer the ball of dough, turning the dough in the bowl to make sure the entire ball of dough is coated. Cover with plastic

continued

wrap and let sit in a warm place for 1 hour, or until doubled in size.

6 Preheat the oven to 450°F. Make sure the rack is in the center of the oven.

7 Dump the dough into the prepared baking pan. Use your fingers to push the dough so that it spreads out to the edges of the entire pan. Cover the pan with plastic wrap and let sit for another 20 minutes.

8 Brush the remaining 2 tablespoons olive oil onto the dough. Using a sharp knife, section off the dough into squares by creating rows first, then creating even squares within the rows. Do not cut through to the bottom, but almost. Make "X" indentions into each of the squares. Sprinkle 1 teaspoon sea salt on top of the dough (if desired).

9 Bake the bread for 15 to 20 minutes, until golden brown.

"Eat little at a time, and only at need. For these things are given to serve you when all else fails. The cakes will keep sweet for many many days, if they are unbroken and left in their leaf-wrappings, as we have brought them. One will keep a traveler on his feet for a day of long labour, even if he be one of the tall Men of Minas Tirith."

—The Fellowship of the Ring

SOFTY CHEESE QUESO

(Inspired by *Adventure Time*)

Jake loves this on a hot dog, but be careful! Overconsumption can lead to spontaneous explosion, and as much as we support eating ALL the cheese, we must caution you! This recipe is packed with flavor and delicious melty goodness—the whole can of queso will be gone in no time if you're not careful.

Prep Time: 5 minutes
Total Time: 25 minutes
Serves: 16 homies

Ingredients

1 poblano pepper

One 14.5-ounce can diced tomatoes

One 32-ounce block Velveeta

¼ cup milk

1 teaspoon onion salt

Instructions

1 Preheat the broiler and line a baking sheet with aluminum foil. Cut the poblano pepper in half, place on the baking sheet, and roast for 3 to 4 minutes, until the outside of the pepper is darkened. Let cool. Remove the skins and seeds and dice the pepper.

2 Drain the can of diced tomatoes and dice further into a small chop.

3 Chop the Velveeta into cubes. Place the cubes and the milk in a large saucepan on medium heat until melted. Add the tomatoes, poblano pepper, and onion salt. Stir until combined and the consistency is runny.

PEETA'S BREAD

(Inspired by *The Hunger Games*)

If you ever find yourself in a dystopian society, eating a hearty loaf like this would provide a moment of respite amidst all that doom and gloom. This bread is loaded with flavor, home cooked comfort, and sweetened by a heavy sprinkling of cranberries, golden raisins, and nuts throughout. It's an anytime bread, perfect when served warm with some butter for breakfast, lunch, or dinner. May the loaves be ever in your favor!

Prep Time: 1 hour 45 minutes
Total Time: 2 hours 5 minutes
Serves: 4 tributes

Ingredients

½ cup rolled oats

3½ cups unbleached bread flour

2 tablespoons granulated sugar

⅓ cup brown sugar

1¼ teaspoons salt

4½ teaspoons active dry yeast

1 tablespoon cinnamon

2 large eggs

2 tablespoons unsalted butter, at room temperature

½ cup milk, at room temperature, plus 1 additional tablespoon

½ cup golden raisins

½ cup dried cranberries

½ cup chopped walnuts

Instructions

1 Boil 1 cup of water in a small saucepan (or microwave in a small heatproof bowl), stir in the oats, and cook for at least 10 minutes, or until all the liquid has disappeared. Set aside.

2 Stir together the flour, both granulated and brown sugars, salt, yeast, and cinnamon in a large mixing bowl. Add 1 egg, the butter, ½ cup of milk, and ¾ cup of room temperature water and stir with a wooden spoon (or on low in a stand mixer with the paddle attachment). Add the oats. Continue to stir on low until the mixture forms into a ball, pulling away from the walls of the bowl. Feel free to adjust by adding a little water or flour in case the dough is too dry or too sticky.

3 Switch to the dough hook attachment and knead on medium speed for about 6 minutes. Lightly flour a surface and gently sprinkle the raisins, cranberries, and walnuts onto the dough and knead by hand for about 2 minutes. The dough should be soft, smooth, and elastic. Grease a large bowl with butter and put the ball of dough in the bowl, turning it

continued

in the bowl to coat with the butter. Cover with plastic wrap and let sit in a warm space for 1 to 2 hours, until doubled in size.

4 Prepare two 9-by-13-inch baking sheets with parchment paper and grease. Divide the dough into two, and roll into long log-shaped loaves. Take the ends and pinch them underneath the loaf to get a good seal. Place each loaf on a pan to proof. Mist the tops with spray oil and cover once again with plastic wrap.

5 Let proof for 30 minutes, or until doubled in size.

6 Preheat the oven to 425°F. Prepare the egg wash by beating the remaining egg and 1 tablespoon of milk. Once the loaves have risen, brush the egg wash on the tops of the loaves and place the pans on the center rack of the oven and bake for 20 to 25 minutes. Spray the sides of the oven with a water bottle (or flick water into the sides of the oven) while cooking to release steam in the oven. The top should be golden brown and the bottom should sound hollow when thumped.

"To this day, I can never shake the connection between this boy, Peeta Mellark, and the bread that gave me hope, and the dandelion that reminded me that I was not doomed."

—The Hunger Games

PIZZA GYOZA

(Inspired by *Teenage Mutant Ninja Turtles*)

Cowabunga to all the turtles, rats, chefs, and more! The Teenage Mutant Ninja Turtles themselves are historically known for their love of pizza, but given the Asian influence on the show, why not take that love and evolve it to the next level? Thus enters the West-meets-East food mash-up you never knew you needed until now. Pan fried with a cheesy base and a pizza surprise in the middle, you've never seen gyoza like this before!

Prep Time: 1 hour
Total Time: 1 hour 15 minutes
Serves: 2 to 4 heroes in a half shell

Ingredients

Dough

2 cups all-purpose flour

1 teaspoon salt

Pizza Filling

2 garlic cloves, minced

1 cup ground Italian sausage

½ cup pepperoni slices

½ cup minced onion

¼ cup shredded mozzarella

½ cup shredded Parmesan

⅓ cup shredded Romano

1 teaspoon fennel

3 tablespoons basil

½ teaspoon freshly ground nutmeg

Pinch of chili flakes

¼ teaspoon salt

½ teaspoon freshly ground black pepper

¼ cup shredded cheese

Dipping Sauce

½ cup black rice vinegar

1 cup soy sauce

½ cup sesame oil

Red chili paste or marinara sauce for serving (optional)

Instructions

1 Sift the flour and 1 teaspoon salt into a medium bowl. Slowly add ½ cup of boiling water, stirring continuously. Continue to add water gradually if dough seems too dry. Roll the dough into a ball and place in a bowl with a damp cloth over it. Let it rise for an hour.

2 Once the dough has risen, punch it down to deflate it and roll out to about ⅛ inch thick on a floured surface. Use a 4-inch circle cookie cutter or a drinking glass as a stencil to cut out your gyoza shapes. Set aside.

continued

3 Combine the garlic, Italian sausage, pepperoni, onion, mozzarella, Parmesan, Romano, fennel, basil, nutmeg, chili flakes, salt, and pepper in a medium bowl. Mix together thoroughly.

4 Scoop out 1 tablespoon of filling and place it in the middle of a gyoza wrapper. Dab your finger in water and wet the outside edge of the wrapper as a glue. Fold it in half, and, beginning on the left side, pleat the two sides of the wrapper all the way around to close it off.

5 In a microwave-safe bowl, combine ⅓ cup water with the ¼ cup shredded cheese and microwave for 30-second intervals until the cheese is melted.

6 In an oiled medium skillet, cook the gyoza on medium-high heat until the bottoms are browned, about 3 minutes. Pour the water-cheese mixture into the pan and cover with a lid, leaving a small opening for the water to evaporate through. The gyoza is done cooking when the majority of the liquid has evaporated. Cut one in half to test if need be.

7 To make the dipping sauce, combine the black rice vinegar, soy sauce, and sesame oil in a small bowl. Mix together. To add extra spiciness, try adding some red chili paste. You can also use marinara sauce as an alternate option.

⚡ *Cheat Code:* You can buy premade gyoza wrappers from your local Asian grocery store or get them online instead of making them from scratch.

MINI PIZZAS

(Inspired by *Back to the Future*)

Back to the Future convinced us that the 21st century would be filled with hoverboards, self-lacing shoes, and fancy food rehydrating machines. Great Scott! None of that technology exists yet (come on, scientists!), but at least we have pizza. These miniature pies are like the sliders of the pizza world—just pick one up and you're on your way to devouring all the best parts of a pizza in one bite.

Prep Time: 1 hour 10 minutes
Total Time: 1 hour 20 minutes
Serves: 16 older versions of yourself

Ingredients

1 recipe Easy Pizza Dough (see page 180) or
    1 package refrigerated pizza dough
¼ cup cornmeal
One 6-ounce can tomato paste
One 8-ounce can tomato sauce
1 tablespoon oregano
½ teaspoon garlic powder
¼ teaspoon onion powder
½ teaspoon salt
½ teaspoon freshly ground black pepper
1 teaspoon granulated sugar
1½ cups shredded mozzarella
½ cup grated Parmesan
3 pepperoni sticks, thinly sliced
1 cup julienned green bell pepper

Instructions

1 Preheat the oven to 425°F. Line a baking sheet with parchment paper and sprinkle with the cornmeal.

2 Prepare the Easy Pizza Dough according to the directions on page 180.

3 Combine the tomato paste and sauce in a small bowl. Mix in the seasonings and the sugar and stir together very well. Set aside. Mix the cheeses together in a small bowl.

4 On a lightly floured surface, roll out the pizza dough to about ¼ inch thick. Make 16 circles out of the pizza dough by using a cookie cutter or a cup as a stencil and cutting around it with a knife. Using a spoon or a cup slightly smaller than your mini crust, indent the middle of the circle. Place the crusts on the cornmeal-covered prepared sheet.

5 Add a teaspoon of sauce and then a light layer of cheese. If needed, chop the shredded cheese in smaller pieces to ensure it fits on the dough rounds. On one half, add a heavy layer of mini pepperonis. On the other side, add the julienned bell peppers.

6 Bake for 10 minutes, or until the crust begins to turn golden brown. Let sit for 5 minutes before serving.

FIRE FLAKES

(Inspired by Avatar: the Last Airbender)

Get them in a pouch and get them in your mouth! Fire Flakes are a staple snack of the Fire Nation, and while they're not spicy enough to make your mouth light on fire, these flakes still pack a punch. The world of Avatar takes so much inspiration from Asian culture that we had to infuse our recipe with the signature flavor of wasabi, which makes these the perfect treat to add some heat to any party or occasion. Flameo, hotman!

Prep Time: 5 minutes
Total Time: 20 minutes
Serves: 4 firebenders

Ingredients

1 teaspoon wasabi powder

½ teaspoon sea salt

½ teaspoon black pepper

½ teaspoon chili powder

½ teaspoon garlic powder

¼ teaspoon paprika

5 cups cornflakes

3 tablespoons sesame oil

Instructions

1 Preheat the oven to 300°F. Line a baking sheet with foil or parchment paper.

2 Mix all the spices together in a small bowl.

3 Pour the cornflakes and sesame oil in a large freezer zipper bag. Toss the cornflakes around to coat in oil. Pour the spices in the bag. Seal and toss to coat once again in the spices.

4 Spread evenly on the baking sheet and bake for 10 to 15 minutes.

BACON-WRAPPED PIGS IN A BLANKET

(Inspired by *Dazed and Confused*)

Whether you're an incoming freshman or a super senior, these bacon-wrapped hot dogs have graduated and got their major in Pigs in a Blanket! Unlike freshman Mitch, you won't need a fake ID to make our beer mustard sauce, which gives each bite a boozy kick.

Prep Time: 25 minutes
Total Time: 40 minutes
Serves: 16 freshmen

Ingredients

8 hot dogs
8 slices thin-cut bacon
One 8-ounce package crescent rolls
2 tablespoons poppy seeds

Beer Spicy Mustard
¼ cup beer (dark or stout)
1½ tablespoons brown sugar
½ cup Dijon mustard
¼ cup yellow mustard

Instructions

❶ Preheat the oven to 375°F. Line a baking sheet with parchment paper or grease with nonstick spray.

❷ Cut the hot dogs in half. Cut the bacon slices in half and wrap one half around each hot dog half. Line them on the baking sheet and bake for 15 minutes, or until the bacon is browned. Let cool for 10 minutes.

❸ Open up the crescent roll dough and cut each perforated triangle in half long ways (from the middle of the triangle to the point) so that there are skinny triangles of dough instead. Do this to all 8 of the crescent dough pieces.

❹ Wrap a crescent dough around each bacon-wrapped hot dog. Once all the hot dogs are wrapped, sprinkle with poppy seeds.

❺ Bake for 10 to 12 minutes, until the dough is golden brown.

- -

"Now fry like bacon, you little freshmen piggies. Fry!"

—*Simone*

6 For the Beer Spicy Mustard: On medium heat, simmer the beer in a small saucepan until the amount is reduced by half, 10 to 15 minutes. Stir in the brown sugar until completely melted. Remove from heat.

7 Allow to cool. Mix in both mustards and pour into a small bowl to serve as a dip for the pigs in the blanket.

CHARCUTERIE PLATE

(Inspired by *Edward Scissorhands*)

Even though having scissorhands seems like it would be a pesky (and pretty dangerous) way to live, we can't help but imagine how much fun it would be to use Edward's sharp fingers to chop-chop-chop the ingredients for this charcuterie plate. This spread is a hit at parties or intimate movie nights. The combination of Cheddar and smoked Gouda with a Lit'l Smokie is both nostalgic and delicious, especially when combined with a side of Garlic Herb Dip and water crackers. Like a grown-up Lunchable!

Prep Time: 30 minutes
Total Time: 35 minutes
Serves: 4 nosy neighbors

Ingredients

One 14-ounce package mini smoked sausages
One 8-ounce package Gouda
One 8-ounce package sharp Cheddar
6 to 10 green olives
1 package water biscuit crackers

Garlic Herb Dip

Two 8-ounce packages cream cheese
¾ cup heavy cream
¼ cup minced fresh chives
4 garlic cloves, finely minced
1 teaspoon dried parsley
½ teaspoon sea salt

Instructions

❶ Fill a small saucepan with 2 to 3 inches of water. Add the mini sausages and simmer for 5 minutes. Take off the heat and set aside to cool.

❷ Cut the Gouda into large cubes and the Cheddar into ¼-inch-thick rectangles. Cut the green olives into slices.

❸ In a medium bowl, combine the Garlic Herb Dip ingredients and stir well. Wrap in plastic wrap and put in the fridge to cool.

❹ Make a stack of a Gouda cube first, then a mini sausage, a Cheddar rectangle, and a green olive slice and spear with a toothpick or sword cocktail pick.

❺ To arrange the charcuterie plate, put the bowl of dip in the middle. Circle the bowl with sausage and cheese spears, and then spread out the water crackers around the spears.

KRONK-WORTHY SPINACH PUFFS

(Inspired by *The Emperor's New Groove*)

This recipe has been described by an Emperor's New Groove food critic as "squeakity squeak, squeak mcsqueakum," which (if our translation is correct) means "very yummy." Kronk, the mislead gentle giant caught up in Yzma's evil-doings, serves this dish with poisoned wine, but we think it pairs better with a nice, nontoxic red vino. Just our opinion! So what are you waiting for? Pull the lever on these stuffed spinach puffs, and watch them disappear off the plate faster than the Emperor's invisible clothes! Hold on, are we mixing up our stories again?

Prep Time: 30 minutes
Total Time: 45 minutes
Serves: 9 Lever Pullers

Ingredients

6 slices bacon

4 ounces cream cheese, room temperature

2 large eggs

1 tablespoon olive oil

½ teaspoon chopped fresh dill

2 cups frozen spinach, chopped, thawed, and water squeezed out

¾ cup crumbled feta

1 onion, finely chopped

Coarse salt

Freshly ground black pepper

1 tablespoon milk

2 sheets (1 box) frozen puff pastry, thawed and cut into 9 squares each

Instructions

❶ Preheat the oven to 400°F. Line a baking sheet with parchment paper.

❷ Cook the bacon in a large skillet over medium heat until slightly crispy. Set on paper towel–lined plate to soak the bacon grease. Chop into small pieces.

❸ Add the softened cream cheese, 1 egg, oil, and dill and mix in a large bowl until combined.

❹ In a separate bowl, combine the spinach, feta, onion, and bacon. Add to the cream cheese mixture and combine to create the filling. Add salt and pepper to taste.

❺ Using the remaining egg, beat into small bowl and mix with milk to create an egg wash.

❻ Spoon a teaspoon of the spinach mixture into the middle of a pastry square. Brush with an egg wash onto opposite edges and fold it diagonally. Use a fork to seal off one end and leave the other end open.

❼ Bake for 13 to 15 minutes, until the puffs are golden brown.

Entrées

SECRET SPAGHETTI SAUCE À LA SCREECH

(Inspired by *Saved by the Bell*)

So many hours of our adolescence were spent in front of the TV watching Saved by the Bell. *Ashley's certainly seen every episode at least twice. So who could forget when Screech shares "his" spaghetti sauce and everyone goes gaga over it? There must be something in the sauce after all the ladies rush him for his autograph! We packed this marinara full of aphrodisiac-inspired ingredients like garlic, chocolate, chili pepper, and sweet basil. Off the wall? Yes. Surprisingly pleasurable to eat? Also yes. You won't want to keep this secret sauce a secret for long.*

Prep Time: 20 minutes
Total Time: 1 hour
Serves: 2 students of Bayside High

Ingredients

1 tablespoon extra virgin olive oil

½ white onion, finely chopped

4 garlic cloves, minced

Two 15-ounce cans crushed tomatoes

One 6-ounce can tomato paste

1 teaspoon chili powder

2 teaspoons milk chocolate or semi-sweet chips

½ teaspoon crushed red pepper

1 teaspoon salt

½ teaspoon freshly ground black pepper

¼ cup chopped fresh sweet basil

Instructions

1 In a large pot or Dutch oven, add the olive oil, onion, and garlic and sauté over medium heat until translucent, 3 to 5 minutes.

2 Add the crushed tomatoes, tomato paste, and ½ cup of water. Stir in the chili powder, chocolate chips, crushed red pepper, salt, and pepper. Bring to a boil and reduce heat to low, cover and simmer for 45 minutes for maximum flavor.

3 Pour into a beaker for aesthetic serving purposes or serve directly over cooked pasta and top with chopped fresh sweet basil.

KRABBY SLIDERS

(Inspired by SpongeBob SquarePants)

ARE YOU READY KIDS? The Krabby Patty is perhaps the most well-known food item in the SpongeBob universe, but the recipe has always been shrouded in mystery. Which is strange, because it just looks like a delicious crab cake hamburger. And the best time for crab cakes is all the time. Since we've got so many customers to serve in Bikini Bottom, we took a crack at some crab cake sliders, slathered in a delicious turmeric tartar sauce aioli. Warning: Once you know the secret recipe, beware of tiny, green, one-eyed geniuses trying to break into your house to steal it.

Prep Time: 30 minutes
Total Time: 40 minutes
Serves: 12 Krusty Krab customers

Ingredients

Turmeric-Tartar Sauce Aioli

1 tablespoon minced onion

¾ cup mayonnaise

2 tablespoons dill pickle relish

1½ tablespoons turmeric

1 tablespoon white wine vinegar

Sea salt and freshly ground black pepper, to taste

Mini Patties

8 ounces shredded imitation or fresh crab meat

1 cup panko bread crumbs

½ cup chopped scallions

2 teaspoons chopped parsley

4 tablespoons mayonnaise

1½ teaspoons Dijon mustard

2 teaspoons Old Bay Seasoning

2 large eggs

Olive oil, for cooking

12 slider hamburger buns

Lettuce

Tomato slices

Gruyère slices

Instructions

1 For the Turmeric-Tartar Sauce Aioli: Add all of the sauce ingredients to a medium mixing bowl and stir to combine well. Place the bowl in the fridge to chill.

2 Mix the crab meat, panko, scallions, parsley, mayonnaise, mustard, and Old Bay Seasoning in a large bowl. Mix in the eggs. Shape the mixture into 12 mini patties about 2 inches in diameter.

3 Heat a large skillet on medium-high heat with a light coat of olive oil and place the patties in the skillet to cook. Cook until golden brown, about 3 minutes per side. Place each side of a bun in the skillet and brown in the same skillet once the patties are done cooking.

4 Spread the aioli on the browned slider buns. Serve with aioli, lettuce, tomato, and Gruyère.

⚡ **Cheat Code:** Using a can of crab meat is an easy alternative to shredded imitation crab meat, and also more affordable.

"The finest eating establishment ever established for eating.
The Krusty Krab, home of the Krabby Patty."

—SpongeBob

PIZZA MAC AND CHEESE

(Inspired by *Home Alone*)

True fans of Home Alone *know that the real reason Kevin McCallister gets left behind is actually because of pizza. Only thing is, if he'd just gotten his cheese slice like he wanted, the world would have been deprived of this amazing movie. In honor of Kevin's insatiable appetite, we've crafted up a dish that combines all of Kevin's favorite foods we see him eat in* Home Alone *and* Home Alone 2.

Prep Time: 15 minutes
Total Time: 30 minutes
Serves: 4 to 6 sticky bandits

Ingredients

2 cups elbow macaroni

1 teaspoon olive oil

1/3 cup heavy cream

1 1/2 cups shredded sharp Cheddar

1/2 teaspoon garlic powder

1/8 teaspoon onion powder

1 cup pizza sauce

1/2 teaspoon Italian seasoning

1 1/2 cups shredded mozzarella

One 6-ounce package sliced pepperoni

Instructions

1 Preheat the oven to 400°F. Grease a large casserole dish.

2 Bring water to a boil in a large pot and cook the macaroni according to package instructions. Add the olive oil to the water to keep the pasta from sticking to one another. Drain the water and set the pasta aside.

3 Return the empty pot to medium heat, add the cream and bring to a soft boil. Add the cheese and spice powders. Stir continuously until the cheese has fully melted and the ingredients are combined to form a smooth cheese sauce. Add the pasta and stir until pasta is coated in cheese. Pour the mac and cheese into the prepared casserole dish.

4 Smooth a thin layer of the pizza sauce over the top of the macaroni. Sprinkle the Italian seasoning over the sauce, followed by half of the mozzarella. Top with a single layer of pepperoni slices, and then sprinkle the rest of the mozzarella on top.

5 Bake for 10 minutes until the cheese is melted. Set oven to broil and broil for 3 to 4 minutes, until the cheese is melted and starting to brown. Let cool before serving.

CHICKEN POTPIE

(Inspired by Roald Dahl's *The Twits*)

Roald Dahl's macabre and darkly comical children's stories left lasting impressions on us. This is our homage. We made sure the basic potpie recipe is mouth-watering on its own; it would be particularly delightful to share with your favorite twit on a cold, dreary day. Inspired by the illustrations of Roald's longtime collaborator Quentin Blake, this pie features bird feet made of toothpicks and skewers. The presentation may horrify your friends, but they will be happy to find bits of crust nestled in their beards for later.

Prep time: 1 hour 15 minutes
Total Time: 1 hour 45 minutes
Serves: 8 to 10 Twits and their victims

Ingredients

⅓ cup all-purpose flour, plus more for rolling out pastry

1 package frozen puff pastry, defrosted

2 boneless chicken breasts

4 tablespoons olive oil

1 russet potato, diced

2 carrots, diced

1 small white onion, diced

3 celery stalks, diced

½ cup frozen peas

2 garlic cloves, minced

2½ cups chicken broth

3 tablespoons white wine vinegar

Salt and freshly ground black pepper

½ cup buttermilk

½ teaspoon dried thyme

½ teaspoon dried rosemary

½ teaspoon dried parsley

1 large egg, beaten

1 tablespoon milk

Instructions

1 Flour a surface for the puff pastry. Sprinkle more flour on top of the pastry and roll it out to one smooth piece of pastry for the top of the potpie. Using kitchen shears or a paring knife, cut out the puff pastry dough in the shape that will cover the top of a 9-inch pie dish. Place the circle on a parchment-lined baking sheet and put in the fridge to chill.

2 Preheat the oven to 425°F.

3 Place the chicken breasts in a large stockpot with about 5 inches of water and bring to a boil over medium heat. Reduce the heat to low, cover and cook for an additional 15 minutes. Drain the chicken and shred. Set aside.

4 Add the olive oil to a large skillet over medium heat. Sauté the potato, carrots, onion, celery, peas, and garlic. Cook until the potato and carrots have softened, 10 to 15 minutes. Add ⅓ cup flour and stir constantly for about 2 minutes. Add the chicken broth, white wine vinegar, and salt and pepper to

continued

taste and bring to a boil, making sure to fully incorporate the flour. Simmer on medium-low until thickened, about 10 minutes.

5 Take off the heat and add the buttermilk, chicken, and seasonings. Ladle the filling into the pie dish. The filling should form a round mound.

6 Prepare an egg wash by mixing the egg and milk. Brush the edge of the pie dish and cover the filling with the puff pastry. Press firmly around the edge of the dish so that the dough adheres to the egg wash. Poke holes in the top of the pie to mark where the chicken feet skewers will go and also to vent the potpie while baking.

7 Bake on a parchment-lined baking sheet for 25 to 30 minutes, until the pastry is golden brown.

8 While baking, create the bird feet. Cut two toothpicks into thirds and glue them to the end of a skewer to resemble a chicken foot. Paint the "feet" with black acrylic paint, leaving 1 to 1½ inches of each skewer unpainted (to stick it into the potpie when finished baking).

GLAMBURGER

(Inspired by *Undertale*)

A specialized burger with purple buns that are also glittery? Can do! The world of Undertale *provides all sorts of intriguing and off-the-wall foods, so we were more than excited to dig deep and figure out how we might pull this colorful recipe off. While the Glamburger in* Undertale *is found in a literal trash can, we're proud to share that our version is pretty much the opposite of that. This bizarre burger tastes as weirdly delicious as it looks. Invite your friends over for dinner and surprise them with these noms—they will never forget it.*

Prep Time: 1 hour 20 minutes
Total Time: 1 hour 45 minutes
Serves: 8 monster souls

Ingredients

2¼ teaspoons (1 envelope) active dry yeast

4 tablespoons granulated sugar

¼ cup warm milk

4 tablespoons (½ stick) butter, melted and cooled

1 large egg, beaten

1 teaspoon salt, plus more for seasoning

5 to 10 drops purple gel food coloring

3½ cups all-purpose flour, plus more for surface

1½ pounds ground chuck

Freshly ground black pepper

1 tablespoon olive oil

Green leaf lettuce

Mayonnaise

Purple luster dust

Purple edible glitter

Instructions

1 Preheat the oven to 400°F. Line a baking sheet with parchment paper.

2 In a large mixing bowl or the bowl of a stand mixer, combine the yeast with 1 cup of warm water and the sugar, milk, and cooled butter. Mix gently and let stand for 5 minutes until foamy.

3 Add the egg and salt, and then add the food coloring drop by drop until you reach the desired shade of purple (note: to obtain a deep color purple, 5 to 10 drops is necessary).

4 With the mixer on low speed, add the flour ½ cup at a time and mix until combined. Increase the speed to medium and continue to beat until dough has elasticity and pulls away from the bowl.

5 On a floured surface, press dough into a disk. With a pastry cutter or a knife, cut into eight equal slices. Flatten each piece with your fingertips and fold the sides over. Pinch the pieces into each other, flip over your ball, and work the ball around in a circle a couple

continued

of times with both of your hands to seal the bottom and to properly shape it. Move the buns to the lined baking sheet and let the dough sit for 15 minutes.

6 Bake the buns for 12 to 15 minutes. When baked, set aside to cool.

7 Meanwhile, make the hamburger patties by diving the ground chuck into eight equal balls. Put a square of wax paper underneath and on top. Press down ball with a plate to flatten the patty. The patty should be about 5 inches in length flattened. Season with the salt and pepper.

8 Add the oil to a large skillet over medium-high heat. Add the patties and cook for 3 to 5 minutes per side, making sure only to flip them once to retain the most flavor.

9 Cut the buns in half horizontally. Place a piece of green leaf lettuce on the bottom bun. Place the patty on top of that with a swirl of mayonnaise and top with the other side of the bun.

10 Garnish the top of the bun with purple luster dust and purple edible glitter.

SHRIMP SCAMPI AND SPINACH PASTA WITH GLAZED CARROTS

(Inspired by *Mrs. Doubtfire*)

Helloooooo! Even though Mrs. Doubtfire's true identity is a scam, this scampi is anything but that! (Eh? Eh?) Dinner is served with this "high class" combination of individual parts that blend well together, and it is certainly better than a Valenti's meal that would've cost you $140 dollars! Plus, you won't have to sit in the smoking section.

Prep Time: 25 minutes
Total Time: 50 minutes
Serves: a single mom and 3 kids

Ingredients

Pasta and Veggies

4 ounces spaghetti

4 ounces spinach (green) spaghetti

1 teaspoon extra virgin olive oil

12 young carrots with stems cut to one inch above carrot

1 tablespoon unsalted butter

1 bunch chives

Edible flowers (optional)

Scampi

2 tablespoons extra virgin olive oil

1 pound shrimp, peeled and deveined

Salt and freshly ground black pepper

2 tablespoons finely chopped shallots

2 garlic cloves, pressed

¼ cup white cooking wine

¼ cup chicken broth

2 tablespoons freshly squeezed lemon juice

2 tablespoons chopped fresh parsley

½ cup heavy cream

½ cup grated Parmesan

2 teaspoons vinegar-based hot sauce

4 tablespoons (½ stick) unsalted butter

continued

Instructions

1 Set a large pot of water to boil and add both the regular spaghetti and spinach spaghetti and cook until al dente, 8 to 12 minutes. Strain and add a teaspoon of olive oil to the pot to keep the pasta from sticking together. Set aside, covered.

2 In a large saucepan, cover the carrots with water and bring to a boil over high heat. Lower the heat to medium and simmer until the carrots are fork tender, 6 to 8 minutes. Remove from the heat and strain. Return the carrots back to the saucepan and add the butter. Let the butter melt, stir gently to coat the carrots. Set aside, covered.

3 To make the scampi, add the 2 tablespoons olive oil and shrimp to a large skillet and cook over medium-high heat until pink, about 3 minutes each side. Remove the shrimp and set on a paper towel–lined plate. Sprinkle with salt and pepper to taste.

4 In the same skillet, cook the shallots and garlic until translucent, 2 to 3 minutes. Pour in the wine, chicken broth, lemon juice, and parsley and simmer for about 5 minutes. Stir in the cream, Parmesan, and hot sauce and simmer until sauce is reduced and begins to thicken, 15 to 20 minutes. Add the ¼ cup butter and stir until melted.

5 Plate the dish by swirling the spaghetti in a circle on one side of the plate. Place a dab of the sauce in the middle of the pasta. Add a large spoonful of the scampi sauce next to the pasta, and place 4 shrimp in the middle of the sauce. Place 3 baby carrots in between the pasta and the shrimp with a long chive in between. Garnish the pasta with an edible flower, if using.

HERRING POTPIE

(Inspired by *Kiki's Delivery Service*)

Of all the things Kiki delivers, herring potpie really stands out in our memories because of its incredible design. In a society where the old is constantly battling against the new, this potpie is a reminder that perhaps we can all still move forward together, bonded by family and food. Now normally when you see a potpie, you think of chicken or beef. This potpie specifically calls for herring, but there is nothing fishy about it! This recipe is surprisingly savory, buttery, flaky, and it's packed with hearty vegetables to make a flavorful filling.

Prep Time: 30 minutes
Total Time: 75 minutes
Serves: 6 aspiring witches

Ingredients

3 sheets frozen puff pastry dough

4 herring fillets (or any white fish)

2½ cups heavy cream

½ cup dry white cooking wine

¼ cup freshly squeezed lemon juice

4 tablespoons (½ stick) unsalted butter

1 small onion, diced

2 large garlic cloves, minced

Salt and freshly ground black pepper

3 tablespoons all-purpose flour

1 cup chopped pumpkin (or Japanese pumpkin or squash)

½ cup chopped carrots

¼ cup diced mushrooms

½ cup corn

1 tablespoon dried dill

3 large eggs

1 tablespoon milk

8 to 12 black olives

Instructions

1 Preheat the oven to 400°F. Grease a large casserole dish.

2 Remove the puff pastry dough from the freezer and set aside to defrost.

3 Place the fish fillets in a large skillet. Mix the heavy cream, white wine, and 1 tablespoon of the lemon juice in a small bowl and pour the wine-cream mixture over the fish until the fish are just covered. Bring the liquid to a boil, cover the fish, and let poach on medium-low heat for 5 to 10 minutes, until the fish becomes firm. Drain the liquid from the fish and keep to add back to the recipe later. Set the fish aside to cool.

4 Add the butter to large skillet and sauté the onion and garlic over medium heat, adding salt and pepper to taste, until the onion becomes clear, about 5 minutes. Add the reserved white wine sauce to the pan and bring to a boil. Add the flour and whisk continuously. The sauce will begin to thicken into gravy.

continued

5 Add the pumpkin, carrots, mushrooms, corn, and dill to the pan to sauté. Break off pieces of the fish and mix them into the sauce as well. Add a dash of salt and pepper. Allow to cook for 5 minutes, or until the mushrooms are tender. Remove from heat.

6 Separate 1 egg and put the yolk aside for later use as the egg wash. Crack the remaining egg into the egg white, beat and lightly fold the eggs into the fish-veggie pie filling. Transfer the filling into the prepared casserole dish. Create an egg wash by combinging the remaining egg yolk plus 1 whole egg with the milk. Brush the edge of the dish with the egg wash to allow the crust to adhere. Set the egg wash aside.

7 Using only one sheet of the puff pastry, place over the dish and trim around the edges of dish. With the second sheet of puff pastry, cut 1-inch strips and lay them diagonally with 1 inch in between each one. Egg wash each strip before placing it, and then egg wash the top of the strips and the spaces in between. Create a fish stencil by drawing a fish on a piece of parchment paper and cut it out with kitchen shears. Gently place the fish stencil on top of the final sheet of puff pastry and cut around it with a paring knife. Don't forget to also cut out the gills and the eyeball. Brush the fish with egg wash and place gills and eyeball on top of the cutout fish. Gently place the fish cutout in the middle and apply more egg wash to the fish to seal the deal. Garnish the top with black olives cut in half, alternating on every other strip.

8 Bake the pie for 25 to 30 minutes; the top should be golden brown. Remove and let cool for at least 15 minutes before serving.

CALZONES

(Inspired by *We Bare Bears*)

The three brother bears often find themselves in crazy situations, and summoning an entire forest of critters and creatures to devour their calzones is honestly among their more sane adventures. We wouldn't blame those animals for going bananas over these calzones—they're filled to the brim with a hearty stuffing and burst at the seams with flavor.

Prep Time: 1 hour 15 minutes
Total Time: 1 hour 45 minutes
Serves: 4 (1 bear-stack plus 1 extra)

Ingredients

1 tablespoon olive oil

1½ cups chopped pancetta

2 cups chopped Italian sausage

2 shallots, chopped

1 cup diced mushrooms

½ teaspoon dried thyme

½ teaspoon freshly ground black pepper

2 tablespoons fresh basil

1 recipe Easy Pizza Dough (see page 180) or
    1 package refrigerated pizza dough

1 cup shredded mozzarella

1 large egg

1 tablespoon milk

Cream Sauce

2 tablespoons unsalted butter

½ cup milk

½ cup heavy cream

2 garlic cloves, minced

Salt

Freshly ground black pepper

¾ cup shredded Parmesan, plus more for sprinkling

¼ cup shredded mozzarella

Instructions

1 Preheat the oven to 375°F.

2 Heat the oil in a large skillet on medium heat. Sauté the pancetta and Italian sausage until browned, about 5 minutes. Add the shallots and sauté for a few more minutes. Add the mushrooms, thyme, and pepper. Keep stirring until the shallots and mushrooms are translucent, about 3 minutes.

3 To make the cream sauce: Melt the butter in a medium saucepan on medium heat. Add the milk, heavy cream, garlic, salt, and pepper to taste. Add the Parmesan and mozzarella and stir until melted. Pour the cream sauce into the pan with the meats and veggies and stir until combined. Chop the fresh basil and set aside all the ingredients.

4 On a lightly floured surface, divide the pizza dough into four pieces. Roll out each piece into a circle about the thickness of a dry lasagna noodle. On each circle, sprinkle one-quarter of the mozzarella cheese and the meat-cream sauce mixture. Sprinkle with additional Parmesan and finally add the basil on top.

5 Prepare an egg wash by beating the egg in a small bowl and mixing it with the milk. Brush the edges of the circles with the egg wash and carefully fold over the calzone, pressing the edges to seal it. Indent little divots around the border with the dull side of a butter knife and (with a sharper knife) three slits on top to vent. Brush the whole thing with the egg wash and let it bake in the oven until golden brown 25 to 30 minutes.

ATOMIC PEPPER CHILI

(Inspired by *Dumb and Dumber*)

When most people think of Dumb and Dumber, *they remember pastel tuxedos, bowl cuts, and quotes so ridiculous they're still funny two decades later. ("We got no food, we got no jobs, our pets' heads are falling off?!") When we at our show,* Feast of Fiction, *think of* Dumb and Dumber, *we think of Harry and Lloyd accidentally murdering someone with atomic chili peppers. Because . . . uh . . . that scene makes us want atomic chili peppers ASAP. Don't worry, we made sure the spice level of this recipe is customizable, so depending on your tolerance for heat, the fire factor is entirely up to you. Speaking of quotes, here's one of Jimmy's all-time favorites: "Big Gulps, huh? ALRIGHT!"*

Prep Time: 25 minutes
Total Time: 1 hour 10 minutes
Serves: 4 to 6 Gas Men

Ingredients

2 pounds ground beef or ground turkey

½ large white onion, chopped

3 garlic cloves, minced

½ green bell pepper, chopped

1 to 3 atomic peppers, minced (based on preferred level of spice)

1 tablespoon extra virgin olive oil

One 6-ounce can tomato paste

2 tablespoons chili powder

1½ teaspoons ground cumin

½ teaspoon ground oregano

½ teaspoon paprika

¼ teaspoon ground cayenne pepper

Salt and freshly ground black pepper

One 15-ounce can kidney beans, drained

One 28-ounce can crushed tomatoes

Instructions

1 Cook the ground beef, onion, garlic, bell pepper, and atomic peppers in the olive oil in a large pot or Dutch oven over medium heat. Cook until the meat is browned, onions are translucent, and peppers are soft, 7 to 10 minutes. Drain the fat from the ground beef and return the beef to the pot. Add the tomato paste, chili powder, cumin, oregano, paprika, and cayenne pepper. Add salt and pepper to taste.

2 Pour in the kidney beans and crushed tomatoes. Stir well to combine. Let the chili come to a boil and reduce heat to low. Cover and let simmer for 45 minutes.

GOTCHA! PORK ROAST

(Inspired by *Food Wars! Shokugeki no Soma*)

Food Wars is a constant source of fictional food inspiration. When Soma is tasked with making a dish with limited ingredients in the kitchen, we never would have guessed it would become one of the most iconic foods ever seen in an anime. This pork roast gets its name from its "gotcha!" factor. From the outside, it looks like a hunk of meat, but GOTCHA! Inside the outer layer of bacon hides potatoes. It's a full meal in one. We love that the potatoes absorb the smoky meat flavor of the bacon, making each bite more foodgasmic than the last.

Prep Time: 25 minutes
Total Time: 60 minutes
Serves: 2 to 3 hungry judges

Ingredients

Pork Roast

3½ russet potatoes, peeled and cubed
1 tablespoon extra virgin olive oil
¾ cup finely chopped onion
¾ cup finely chopped Eringi mushrooms
Salt and freshly ground black pepper to taste
Two 12-ounce packages thick-cut bacon
2 to 3 sprigs fresh rosemary
Watercress for garnish

Sauce

½ cup red cooking wine
Sweet sake soy sauce
2 tablespoons unsalted butter

Instructions

1 Preheat the oven to 300°F.

2 Steam the potatoes in a large pot for 10 to 12 minutes, until they are soft. Mash the potatoes with a fork or potato masher. Set aside.

3 In a medium skillet, add the olive oil and sauté the onion and Eringi mushrooms until tender and translucent, 8 to 10 minutes. Add the sautéed veggies to the mashed potatoes and combine. Add salt and pepper to taste.

4 On a parchment- or foil-lined baking pan, prepare a bacon wrap by laying out bacon strips and alternately weaving the strips of bacon through every other strip of bacon.

5 Mold the mashed potatoes into a loaf-like shape. Place the loaf on top the bacon strips and carefully wrap the bacon around it, one bacon strip at a time. You might need to add strips to the ends and on top in

continued

case your bacon wrap is not long enough to cover the entire potato roast. Use twine or thin string to tightly wrap the roast so as to not fall apart while baking.

6 Break off pieces of rosemary into small sprigs and sporadically stick them into the strings of the roast.

7 Bake for 35 to 45 minutes, until the bacon is golden brown. Broil on high for 3 minutes to make it extra crispy.

8 While the roast is baking, prepare the sauce: Combine the cooking wine, soy sauce, and butter in a small skillet and reduce for 5 to 7 minutes over medium heat.

9 Remove the pork roast from the oven. Cut off the string, pour the red wine glaze on top, and garnish with watercress.

PINEAPPLE-PORK FRIED RICE

(Inspired by Food Wars! Shokugeki no Soma)

Well, we did it. We've schemed up the most pineapply pineapple fried rice recipe of all time. Thank you, thank you! We're sure Soma would approve. This dish contains pineapple, is baked in a pineapple, and is then shaped like a pineapple. However, it won't turn you into a pineapple (that we know of). Amaze your friends with this visually stunning and mouth-wateringly delicious fried rice at a dinner party. Just sit back and watch as their minds (and maybe their clothes) are blown off in delight.

Prep Time: 35 minutes
Total Time: 55 minutes
Serves: 4 passionate taste testers

Ingredients

1 whole pineapple (including pineapple shell and leaves)

1 tablespoon sea salt, plus more if needed

2 tablespoons coconut oil

1 cup ground pork

½ cup diced white onion

2 carrots, peeled and diced

1 tablespoon oyster sauce

2½ cups cooked white rice

1 tablespoon curry powder

1 teaspoon soy sauce

Pinch of freshly ground black pepper

2 large eggs

⅓ cup frozen peas

2 scallions, sliced

Instructions

1. Preheat the oven to 300°F.

2. Cut off the stem of the pineapple, setting the leaves aside. Cut the pineapple in half vertically.

3. Scoop out the pineapple and dice the flesh into chunks. Sprinkle the sea salt inside both sides of the pineapple shell. Set aside.

4. Heat 1 tablespoon of the coconut oil in a large skillet or wok over medium heat. Add the ground pork and cook until browned, about 5 minutes. Add the pineapple, onion, and carrots. Stir-fry until the carrots are tender, and the onions are soft, 8 to 10 minutes. Add the oyster sauce. Stir the cooked white rice into the skillet, making sure the rice isn't clumpy and the mixture is well combined. Add the curry powder, soy sauce, and pepper. Continue to cook until the curry is fragrant and the rice is shiny, about 5 minutes.

continued

5 In a separate small skillet, add the remaining tablespoon of coconut oil and scramble the eggs for 1 to 2 minutes until they are three-quarters of the way cooked. Combine the eggs with the pork and veggies, along with the peas and scallions, and mix to combine.

6 Transfer the fried rice from the skillet to the inside of the pineapple shells and bake on a baking sheet for 20 minutes. Take out of the oven to cool.

7 Fill up a large oval bowl with your fried rice and pack it in tight to resemble the inside of the pineapple. Place a larger plate or serving dish on top of the bowl and flip the bowl over. Add the pineapple stem to the top of the fried rice to complete the look.

"This dish has advanced Chinese cuisine."

—Orie Sendawara

TIANA'S GUMBO

(Inspired by *The Princess and the Frog*)

If you're getting a big group of people together, there's no better way to bond them than over a steaming pot of gumbo. It's quintessential Cajun cooking for a reason! Our recipe includes shrimp, andouille, and absolutely no frog legs. It's packed with veggies, and we dream of Tiana adding our homemade Cajun seasoning to her menu.

Prep Time: 35 minutes
Total Time: 1 hour 35 minutes
Serves: 8 to 10 bayou amphibians

Ingredients

8 tablespoons (1 stick) unsalted butter
½ cup all-purpose flour
1 cup diced onion
2 teaspoons minced garlic
1 cup chopped red bell pepper
2 celery stalks, diced
1 bay leaf
¼ teaspoon ground white pepper
¼ teaspoon ground black pepper
½ teaspoon cayenne pepper
½ teaspoon dried thyme
½ teaspoon dried oregano
3 cups chicken broth
One 14.5-ounce can diced tomatoes
1 cup frozen sliced okra, thawed
1 pound andouille sausage, thinly sliced
1 pound shrimp, peeled and deveined
1 cup cooked rice
Hot sauce

Instructions

1 In a large stockpot over medium heat, melt the butter. Create a roux by adding the flour to the melted butter, whisking constantly until golden brown. It's critical to be mindful of how fast or slow the roux is cooking. If it's cooking too quickly, take it off the heat for a couple seconds and keep stirring, then return to the burner. The roux is the most important, flavorful part of a gumbo, so be extra careful not to let it burn, or you will have to start over. Cook for around 10 minutes to achieve the richness in flavor.

2 Stir in the onion, garlic, bell pepper, celery, bay leaf, all three peppers, thyme, and oregano. Stir continuously until the mixture is combined and the vegetables are coated.

3 Add 2 cups of water, the chicken broth, and diced tomatoes. Stir in the okra and sausage. Bring to a boil. Reduce the heat to a simmer and let cook for 30 minutes for all of the flavors to fully absorb.

4 Add the shrimp, cover, and cook for 30 more minutes.

5 Serve over cooked rice with a side of hot sauce.

HAZELNUT SOUP

(Inspired by *Tangled*)

Mother knows best, and she certainly has this recipe on lockdown. It's become Rapunzel's favorite dish after years of solitude. We're just glad that Rapunzel got to at least eat well while she was holed up in that tower. Imagine how rough things would have been if Mother Gothel was a bad cook! This soup is so comforting after a long day. Definitely throw this together, let down your hair, and take some time to relax.

Prep Time: 30 minutes
Total Time: 1 day 30 minutes
Serving Size: 2 imprisoned princesses

Ingredients

2 cups hazelnuts

¼ teaspoon salt

1 cup diced parsnips

1½ cups diced butternut squash

½ cup diced onion

4 tablespoons (½ stick) unsalted butter

1 cup vegetable broth

1 cup half-and-half

Cinnamon for garnish

Edible flowers for garnish

Instructions

1 Soften the hazelnuts by soaking them overnight in water in a large bowl.

2 Drain the water and add the hazelnuts to a food processor or a bowl and use an immersion blender. Add 2 cups of water and the salt and pulse until the hazelnuts are pureed.

3 Strain the liquid from the hazelnut puree with a cheesecloth into a large bowl (this liquid is hazelnut milk). Set the milk aside and dispose of the hazelnuts.

4 Dice the parsnips, butternut squash, and onion.

5 Melt the butter in a large saucepan over medium heat. Add the diced veggies. Stir in the vegetable broth, half-and-half, and the reserved hazelnut milk and allow to simmer for 20 minutes, or until the vegetables have softened to fork tender. Remove the soup from the heat.

6 Pour the contents of the saucepan back into the food processor and blend until it is a smooth and creamy consistency.

7 Serve in a bowl with a sprinkle of cinnamon and an edible flower as a garnish.

Desserts

BUTTERSCOTCH CINNAMON PIE

(Inspired by *Undertale*)

Which do you prefer, butterscotch or cinnamon? Why not both! When Toriel made us this HP-restoring delight, we all wished it was real. Creating a recipe from scratch might seem like an impossible task when all you have to go off of is a tiny pixelated image in a videogame. But the moment the words butterscotch, cinnamon, and pie were combined together, we knew we'd be doing the world a disservice not to bring it to real life. This pie is like an ooey gooey butterscotch cinnamon explosion, finished off with a flaky crust and a cute but simple 8-bit heart design to fill us with . . . DETERMINATION.

Prep Time: 3 hours
Total Time: 7 hours
Serves: 8 humans low on HP

Ingredients

1 recipe Piecrust (see page 175) or 1 frozen or
    refrigerated ready-made piecrust
1 teaspoon sea salt
6 tablespoons unsalted butter
2 cups brown sugar
1½ cups heavy cream
¼ cup cornstarch
3 egg yolks
1½ teaspoons vanilla extract
1½ teaspoons cinnamon

Instructions

1 Preheat the oven to 375°F.

2 Set the piecrust into an 9-inch pie dish, cut off the excess dough and set aside, and chill in the freezer for 10 to 15 minutes. When cooled, remove from the freezer and dock the piecrust with a fork. Line the piecrust with parchment paper and fill the dish with dry beans. Blind-bake for 15 minutes. Remove the parchment and beans and bake for another 10 minutes until the crust is golden brown. Cool and set aside.

3 Prepare an 8-bit heart design by rolling out the piecrust scraps. On a floured surface, roll out the dough to about the thickness of a lasagna noodle and use a small (½-inch) square cookie cutter to cut out as many small squares and 1-inch pieces (the size of two squares) of dough as you can. Bake on a parchment-lined baking sheet for 5 to 8 minutes, until golden brown.

continued

4 While the crust is baking, prepare the filling. Combine the salt, butter, and brown sugar in a large saucepan. Bring to a boil over medium heat until the mixture gets to the soft-crack stage (270 to 290°F), about 10 minutes. Add the heavy cream and cornstarch. While stirring continuously, bring to a slow boil to thicken. Cook until the mixture coats the back of a spoon. Remove from heat.

5 In a medium bowl, whisk the egg yolks and pour about one-quarter of the mixture from the saucepan into the eggs in a slow, consistent stream, stirring constantly to temper the eggs. Pour the contents of the bowl back into the saucepan and stir until thickened, about 5 minutes. Remove from heat. Stir in the vanilla and cinnamon.

6 Pour the filling into the cooled crust immediately and place the crust squares on the pie in the shape of an 8-bit heart. Refrigerate for at least 4 hours.

GIANT OATMEAL CREME PIE

(Inspired by *Honey, I Shrunk the Kids*)

Sometimes you just gotta go big or go home—or in this case, get shrunk and try to find your way home! You might feel the urge to grab handfuls of this creme filling or take a huge bite out of it yourself—either way you'll be making a statement when this giant concoction lands on the table. The upside to making a dessert this big is that you won't have to undergo an accidental science experiment and get shrunk to a tiny size before indulging in all this creme pie has to offer.

Prep Time: 15 minutes
Total Time: 1 hour
Serves: 12 to 16 shrunken kiddos

Ingredients

3½ cups all-purpose flour

2½ cups old-fashioned oats

2½ teaspoons baking powder

2½ teaspoons cornstarch

1 teaspoon salt

4 teaspoons cinnamon

2 teaspoons nutmeg

1 pound (4 sticks) unsalted butter, softened

2½ cups granulated sugar

4 tablespoons molasses

2 teaspoons vanilla extract

3 large eggs

Marshmallow Buttercream Filling

¾ pound (3 sticks) unsalted butter

Two 7-ounce jars marshmallow creme

4 cups confectioners' sugar

2 teaspoons vanilla extract

3 tablespoons heavy cream

Instructions

1 Preheat the oven to 350°F. Line a 13-inch round pizza baking pan with parchment paper.

2 In a large bowl, mix the flour, oats, baking powder, cornstarch, salt, cinnamon, and nutmeg. Set aside.

3 In a large mixing bowl or in the bowl of a stand mixer with the paddle attachment, cream the butter. Add the sugar and molasses and whip until creamy. Add vanilla and stir to combine.

4 Incorporate the eggs one at a time, making sure the one before it is combined before adding the next. Scrape down the sides of the bowl with a spatula and continue mixing.

5 Turn the mixer on low and slowly add the dry ingredients. Mix until well combined.

6 Divide the dough in two. Form one half of the dough into a disk about 1½ inch thick, making sure there will be at 3 inches of clearance around the pizza pan for it to spread. Bake for 10 minutes. Take the pan

continued

out of the oven and slam the dough on a countertop 3 to 5 times to deflate the dough and create cracks. Put the dough back in the oven for an additional 10 minutes to finish baking until the edges are golden brown. Allow to cool to room temperature. Repeat this process with other half of the dough, making sure to shape both halves as similar as possible.

7 While the cookies are baking, prepare the filling by adding the 3 sticks of butter and marshmallow creme to the bowl of a stand mixer and whipping until fluffy.

8 Add the confectioners' sugar in increments until fully combined. Scrape down the sides of the bowl with a spatula to fully incorporate.

9 Add the vanilla and heavy cream and beat until smooth and fluffy.

10 After both of the cookies have cooled, place one of the cookies bottom side up on serving tray. Spoon out the filling onto the cookie in a mound that stops 1 inch away from the edge of the cookie. Place the other cookie right side up on top of it and press gently to move filling to the edges of the cookie.

⚡ *Cheat Code:* You can put the icing into a gallon-sized zip-top bag, snip off the corner, and, starting in the middle of the cookie, pipe all the way around the cookie to get a really nice application of the frosting.

FRUIT PIES

(Inspired by *Avatar: The Last Airbender*)

Water. Earth. Fire . . . Fruit pies. Seriously, these are so good, you will be inhaling them like air. The airbenders in Avatar use the power of the elements to take this recipe to the next level, and we're prepared to elevate it as well. Since we don't have airbending capabilities (that we know of), the secret source of our power is cheesecake. So, guess you can call us piebenders from now on, thank you very much.

Prep Time: 20 minutes
Total Time: 1 hour, 40 minutes
Serves: 6 air nomads

Ingredients

1½ cups crushed graham cracker crumbs

5 tablespoons unsalted butter, melted

Two 8-ounce packages cream cheese, at room
    temperature

2/3 cup granulated sugar

1/3 cup heavy cream

2 large eggs

1 teaspoon vanilla extract

1 teaspoon strawberry jam

1 teaspoon blueberry jam

1 teaspoon orange marmalade

1 teaspoon lemon curd

Colored Whipped Cream

½ cup heavy cream

1 tablespoon granulated sugar

Gel food coloring (pink, purple, orange, yellow)

Instructions

1 Preheat the oven to 325°F.

2 In a medium bowl, mix the graham cracker crumbs and melted butter in a bowl until well combined. Pack down the crumb mixture in the bottom of a rectangle cake pan to create crust. Put in the freezer for 10 minutes to set.

3 Once the crust has hardened, use a round cookie cutter or glass that is the size of the openings in a silicone muffin pan to cut six circle crusts. Set these aside.

4 In a medium bowl or in the bowl of a stand mixer, beat the cream cheese and sugar until combined. On low speed, add the heavy cream, eggs, and vanilla. Pour the mixture into the muffin pan, filling the wells about two-thirds of the way up. Drop a dollop of jam into the middle of each (you can make all the same flavor or use any flavor combination you prefer). Cover the jam with more cream cheese mixture and fill almost all the way to the top, leaving room to cover the mixture with the graham cracker crust circle.

continued

5 Set the silicone muffin pan in a 9-by-13-inch baking dish and fill it up with hot water halfway up the sides of the silicone muffin mold, creating a bain-marie. Bake for 20 to 25 minutes, or until the center is set. Cool to room temperature before placing in the freezer to chill for at least 1 hour.

6 While the pies are freezing, make the whipped cream by whipping the heavy cream and sugar in a mixer until it reaches soft peaks. Divide the whipped cream into four bowls and color each bowl to match the flavors of each fruit pie, and continue to hand mix until the peaks become stiff.

7 Once the fruit pies have frozen, place the graham cracker crusts on to each pie and press down firmly. Carefully remove the pies from the silicone muffin pan by flipping them onto a plate, crust side down. Pipe or spoon a dollop of colored whipped cream onto each of the pies before serving.

8-BIT CAKE

(Inspired by *Minecraft*)

Growing up, we built vast imaginary worlds with Legos and Lincoln Logs. These days, kids and kids-at-heart satisfy that creative itch with very different building blocks—in Minecraft. *But whether you're dodging creepers online or daydreaming about colorful plastic brick houses, we recommend you build up an appetite for this eye-catching cake. The pixel-perfect shape is iconic, while the decadent red velvet cake inside is a major crowd-pleaser. Your hunger bar will be full, and your inner architect will thank you.*

Prep Time: 2 hours
Total Time: 2 hours 45 minutes
Serves: 24 creepers

Ingredients

¾ pound (3 sticks) unsalted butter, plus more for preparing pans

3½ cups granulated sugar

6 large eggs

5 teaspoons unsweetened cocoa powder

4 teaspoons vanilla extract

Red gel food coloring

2 cups buttermilk

5 cups all-purpose flour

4½ teaspoons baking powder

2 teaspoons salt

2 recipes Cream Cheese Buttercream (see page 178)

Red, gray, and brown sugar sheets

Instructions

1 Grease two 8-inch square pans with butter and line parchment paper.

2 Preheat the oven to 350°F.

3 In a large bowl or in the bowl of a stand mixer, add the butter and sugar and cream until combined. Add the eggs one at a time, making sure each one is incorporated before adding the next one. Add the cocoa powder, vanilla extract, and red food coloring. Mix until combined. Finally, add the buttermilk, flour, baking powder, and salt and mix until the batter is smooth.

4 Fill the two pans about three-quarters full and bake for 25 to 30 minutes, or until a toothpick comes out clean. Let the cakes cool completely. Once cool, remove cakes from the pans and set aside.

5 Re-grease your pans and line them again with parchment paper. Bake the rest of the remaining batter in three more batches, giving you five layers of cake in total.

continued

6 Prepare a double-batch of the Cream Cheese Buttercream, following the instructions on page 178.

7 Once all of the cakes have cooled, trim the tops of each cake with a bread knife to create even cake layers.

8 Spread a thin layer of frosting on your serving dish to keep the cake in place. Place one cake layer down, adding a layer of frosting in between (use an ice cream scoop to keep the frosting between the layers consistent). Once all of the layers are stacked, stick four straws into the cake and trim to the length of the cake to keep the cake layers in place. Crumb-coat the cake by covering the entire cake with a thick layer of frosting to seal in all of the crumbs and put in the fridge for at least 45 minutes to set.

9 Once the crumb coat is set, add another layer of frosting to cover up the layer of icing before it. Smooth the sides with a smoother or offset spatula to get sharp edges. Repeat the step above if necessary, until the frosting is free of crumbs and the surface is smooth and white.

10 Cut the brown sugar sheets to resemble a pattern that looks like a castle wall with alternating height squares (see photo on page 123). This will go on the bottom of the cake. You need four cutouts, one for each side of the cake. Before applying, cut the gray brown sugar sheets into small, even rectangles to fit around the squares of the brown sugar sheets, acting as an 8-bit shadow. Using the red sugar sheets, cut out the different sized squares that will go on the top of the cake.

⚡ *Cheat Code:* If those sugar sheets are hard to find, fondant is an easy and effective replacement.

APPLE TART WITH RASPBERRY JAM

(Inspired by *The Hobbit*)

If we told you Dwarves have some of the heartiest appetites in all of Middle-earth, would you be surprised? All that mining must be hungry work. Honestly, we kind of relate, because we're always in the mood for a Shire-style brunch. When faced with feeding a gaggle of ravenous Dwarves in The Hobbit, Bilbo whips out some tasty-sounding pastries, so we are following in his hairy little footsteps. Inspired by Bifur the Dwarf, this Hobbit-sized tart is the perfect addition to any brunch or dessert, especially when it's topped with a scoop of vanilla ice cream. The sweetness of the jam, tart crisp apple slices, and a flaky galette-style crust are all you need to turn the nose of every other hungry adventurer nearby. Thanks for the pastry lesson, Bilbo!

Prep Time: 2 hours 40 minutes
Total Time: 3 hours
Serves: 6 Dwarves in their stone halls

Ingredients

1 Tart Crust recipe (see page 175) or 1 refrigerated
   ready-made piecrust

4 large apples, peeled, cored, and thinly sliced
   (about ⅛ inch)

¼ cup granulated sugar, plus more for sprinkling

2 teaspoons lemon juice

2 teaspoons lemon zest

6 tablespoons raspberry preserves

Instructions

1 Prepare the Tart Crust recipe according to the instructions on page 175, or remove the ready-made dough from the fridge. On a lightly floured surface, roll out the dough to about ⅛ inch thick and cut out 6-inch rounds using either a cookie cutter or cutting around a bowl with a knife. Feel free to use crust scraps and re-roll to create enough rounds. Place the rounds on a parchment paper–lined baking sheet and chill in the refrigerator for at least 20 minutes.

2 Cut the apple slices in half crosswise. Toss them in a large bowl with the sugar, lemon juice, and zest.

3 Preheat the oven to 400°F.

continued

4 Take the rounds out of the fridge. Place a tablespoon of the raspberry preserves in the middle of each circle. Spread the jam around the dough leaving an inch border around the edge.

5 Fan the apples slices on top of the jam in a cascading pattern all the way around until it makes a circle. Fold the edges of the dough over the apples and press firmly to seal after each fold. Chill again in the refrigerator for 20 minutes.

6 Brush the edges with water and sprinkle with sugar. Bake for 20 to 22 minutes, until golden brown. Let cool.

"'I hope there is something left for the late-comers to eat and drink! What's that? Tea! No thank you! A little red wine, I think, for me.' 'And for me,' said Thorin. 'And raspberry jam and apple-tart,' said Bifur."

—The Hobbit

CHER-ABLE COOKIES

(Inspired by *Clueless*)

Clueless was a coming-of-age movie of epic proportions for a teenage girl growing up in the '90s. And let's face it, we've all had our moments in the kitchen when we vacuum up everything in sight. Now, real foodies (or just us crazy folks at Feast of Fiction*) might ask the question: How much of an actual heifer would we be if we threw all those things together as the ultimate mash-up? Thus, our own Cher-able Cookies were born. It's an amalgamation of flavors that miraculously works just right together. Salty and sweet peanut butter M&M's meet the crunchiness of popcorn and Special K, and candied turkey bacon adds that je ne sais quoi. Oh, and don't ask about the licorice—as if we'd ever be crazy enough to put licorice in a cookie, gosh!*

Prep Time: 45 minutes
Total Time: 55 minutes
Serves: 22 Betties and Baldwins

Ingredients

Candied Turkey Bacon
¼ cup brown sugar
½ cup maple syrup
8 slices turkey bacon

For the cookies
½ pound (2 sticks) unsalted butter
½ cup brown sugar
⅔ cup granulated sugar
1 large egg
1 teaspoon vanilla extract
2 cups all-purpose flour
½ teaspoon baking soda
½ teaspoon baking powder
1½ teaspoons salt
2 cups crushed Special K cereal
⅔ cup crushed Peanut Butter M&M's
½ cup popped and crushed popcorn

Instructions

1 Preheat the oven to 350°F. Line a baking sheet with parchment paper or foil, or use a baking rack over a baking sheet. Line another baking sheet with parchment paper.

2 Mix ¼ cup brown sugar and the syrup in a small bowl. Dip the bacon strips into the sugar syrup. Line them on the baking sheet and bake for 8 minutes, then flip bacon to the other side and bake for 8 more. Let cool, chop into very small pieces, and set aside.

3 In the bowl of a stand mixer or in a large bowl with a hand mixer, combine the butter, ½ cup brown sugar, and granulated sugar, and cream together for about 2 minutes at medium speed. Scrape the sides of the bowl with a spatula and add the egg and vanilla extract. Continue to mix for about 5 more minutes.

4 Reduce the mixing speed to low, add the flour, baking soda, baking powder, and salt. Mix only until just combined.

continued

5 Using a wooden spoon, mix in the Special K cereal, M&M's, popcorn, and crumbled turkey bacon. Don't overmix the batter.

6 Using an ice cream scoop (or about 1½ tablespoons of cookie dough), scoop the dough onto the lined cookie sheet with at least 3 inches of space between each cookie.

7 Bake for 10 to 12 minutes, until the sides of the cookie begin to brown. (Remember, cookies continue to bake for a couple of minutes after being taken out of the oven while cooling, so don't overbake.)

"I feel like such a heifer. I had two bowls of Special K, three pieces of turkey bacon, a handful of popcorn, five peanut butter M&M's, and three pieces of licorice."

—Cher Horowitz

CHICKEN AND METH CUPCAKES

(Inspired by *Breaking Bad*)

Sometimes a Feast of Fiction recipe is a faithful interpretation of what we see on our screens, and other times we're inspired to come up with something entirely unique and amazing on its own. Breaking Bad is one of those shows that blew us all away, and it's only fitting we devised a recipe that could evoke its most iconic elements—and be the talk of the party for any occasion. Whether you're making them for family or friends, these cupcakes will delight the imagination as you bite into what looks just like a fried chicken wing to be rewarded with a crunchy caramel candy surprise. Look, if Walter White could use chemistry to turn one thing into another, who says we can't transform a regular cupcake into a mouthwatering bucket of fried chicken?

Prep Time: 40 minutes
Total Time: 1 hour
Serves: 12 "cooks"

Ingredients

½ pound (2 sticks) plus 2 tablespoons unsalted butter

1¼ cups granulated sugar

3 large eggs

2½ teaspoons vanilla extract

2¼ cups all-purpose flour

2½ teaspoons baking powder

½ teaspoon salt

½ cup plus 5 tablespoons milk

1 recipe Swiss Meringue Buttercream (see page 179)

12 mini marshmallows

¾ cup white chocolate chips

12 pretzel sticks

2 teaspoons coconut oil

1 cup corn flakes

18 soft caramels

Blue sugar rock sprinkles

Instructions

1 Preheat the oven to 350°F. Line a 12-cup muffin tin with cupcake liners, line a small baking sheet with parchment paper, and line a large baking sheet with parchment paper.

2 Cream the butter and sugar in a large bowl or the bowl of a stand mixer. Beat in the eggs one at a time. Stir in the vanilla extract.

3 In a separate medium bowl, combine the flour, baking powder, and salt. Slowly add to the butter and sugar mixture and mix until combined. Stir in ½ cup plus 2 tablespoons milk (the remaining 3 tablespoons are used later) until the batter is smooth. Fill the cupcake liners about three-quarters full. Pour the rest of the batter into the small lined baking sheet. Bake both the pans for 15 to 22 minutes, being sure to test the cupcakes with a toothpick, and cooking the cake

continued

in the pan until golden brown. Let the cupcakes and cake cool.

4 While the cakes are baking, mix up a batch of the Swiss Meringue Buttercream frosting according to the instructions on page 179.

5 Crush up the cake in the baking sheet into a large bowl. Add frosting by the tablespoon until the consistency equals wet sand, 3 to 4 tablespoons. On a parchment-lined baking sheet, mold the mixture into 12 fried chicken–shaped cake pops (about ¾ inch long).

6 Cut the mini marshmallows in half with kitchen-safe scissors.

7 Melt ¼ cup of the white chocolate chips in the microwave in 30-second increments until melted. Dip 1 inch of side of a pretzel stick in the melted chocolate and then stick this side of the pretzel into the narrower part of the chicken-shaped balls (creating the drumstick). Dip the other side of the pretzel stick into the white chocolate and stick the mini marshmallow halves back together on each side of the pretzel (the chocolate will act as glue to create a chicken bone). Line the "drumsticks" on a clean lined baking sheet and put in the fridge for at least 15 minutes, or until set.

8 Melt the remaining ½ cup white chocolate chips in the microwave in 30-second intervals (about two intervals—stirring in between each one). Add the coconut oil and stir. Pour the mixture into a lowball glass or coffee mug. (You want the chocolate to come up high enough to cover the "bone" of the chicken leg.) Holding on to the cake chicken, dip the pretzel-marshmallow combo into the cup up to the cake pop. Return the drumsticks to the baking sheet and put back in the fridge to set a final time.

9 Crush the corn flakes in a food processor or put them in a zip-top bag and crush them with a rolling pin. Put them in a shallow bowl and set aside.

10 Place the caramels in a double broiler on the stove over medium heat. Mix in the remaining 3 table-spoons milk and stir until the caramels are melted and the mixture is completely combined. Dip the chicken-shaped cake pop into the caramel, swirl the drumstick around to get rid of excess caramel, and immediately dip into the bowl of crushed corn flakes, covering all of the caramel (this is what gives your chicken the fried appearance). Let them set on the baking sheet one final time before decorating.

11 Ice the cupcakes with the Swiss Meringue Buttercream, place a candy drumstick on the cupcake, and scatter bits of blue sugar rock sprinkles on the frosting areas.

⚡ *Cheat Code:* You can always buy cupcakes from your local grocery store or bakery and put the cake-pop chicken wings and blue rock candy on top. We won't snitch!

WELCOME HOME CAKE

(Inspired by *Coraline*)

We'd personally feel more comfortable if this towering and impressive Welcome Home Cake wasn't presented in such creepy circumstances, but leave it to Laika to take the idea of what's normally a source of comfort and happiness and turn it on its head. You're more than welcome to tailor this cake to any occasion, so go ahead and scribble anything you'd like on the top! Just don't forget that mother is always watching . . .

Prep Time: 45 minutes
Total Time: 2 hours
Serves: 12 to 16 "other" children

Ingredients

Butter for greasing pans

1 recipe Devil's Food Cake (see page 177)

1 recipe Swiss Meringue Buttercream (see page 179)

4 ounces semisweet chocolate

Yellow fondant

Red gel decorating icing

Pink candles

Strawberry Ganache

½ cup heavy cream

1½ cups white chocolate chips

Pink food gel coloring

½ teaspoon strawberry extract

Instructions

1 Preheat the oven to 350°F. Grease two 8-inch cake pans with butter and line with parchment paper.

2 Bake the Devil's Food Cake according to the instructions on page 177. Let the cake cool completely.

3 While the cake is baking, make the Swiss Meringue Buttercream according to the instructions on page 179.

4 Melt the semisweet chocolate in a microwave-safe bowl for 30 seconds and let cool. When the chocolate is room temperature, fold it into the Swiss Meringue Buttercream.

5 Stack the cakes on top of each other with a heavy layer of chocolate frosting in between them. Then ice the rest of the cake and put it in the fridge to set.

6 To create the ganache, pour the heavy cream into a small saucepan over medium heat. Remove the pan when the cream starts to simmer.

continued

7 Place the white chocolate chips into a medium bowl and quickly pour the hot cream into the bowl. Let the mixture sit undisturbed for 3 minutes before stirring. After 3 minutes, stir the ganache and add pink gel color by the drop to desired color. Stir in the strawberry extract. Let it cool to room temperature, but don't let it sit too long or it will become too thick and not ideal for dripping.

8 Pull the cake out of the fridge and use a spoon to drip the ganache down the sides of the cake all the way around. Pour the remaining ganache in the middle and smooth. Put the cake in the fridge to cool.

9 Create fondant flowers out of the yellow fondant using a flower stamp or by hand. Make a hole in the middle of each flower using a straw.

10 Place the fondant flowers around the top of the cake. Write "Welcome Home!" or any other greeting that you like in the center with the red gel icing.

11 Place pink candles in the center of each flower and enjoy!

IMAGINATION PIE

(Inspired by *Hook*)

There is something pure and wholesome about the iconic scene in Hook *when the Lost Boys use their imagination to create an epic feast. Sometimes, the real magic in life lies in those rare moments when you can rid yourself of your preconceived notions and take the plunge to believing in something greater than reality. This scene is a true Feast of Fiction—so we brought imagination to reality by creating a light and fluffy coco-strawberry cream pie that's lurking underneath the bright and colorful exterior. This pie is rich in flavor thanks to the infusion of dried strawberries and coconut extract. Now let your imagination run wild, take flight, and dive into this recipe before any scallywag pirates can get their hooks into it.*

Prep Time: 3 hours 35 minutes
Total Time: 7 hours 35 minutes
Serves: 6 to 8 Lost Boys

Ingredients

Coconut-Strawberry Cream Pie

1 recipe Piecrust (see page 175) or 1 refrigerated
    ready-made piecrust
5 large egg yolks
2/3 cup granulated sugar
1/4 cup all-purpose flour
2 cups heavy cream
One 14-ounce can coconut cream
1/2 cup dried strawberries, powdered
1 tablespoon lemon zest
1 cup shredded coconut

Whipped Cream Topping

4 cups heavy cream
3 tablespoons granulated sugar
1/2 teaspoon coconut extract
Red, orange, blue, and green gel food coloring

Instructions

1 Prepare the Piecrust according to the instructions on page 175 or remove the ready-made piecrust from the fridge. Place the crust into 9-inch pie dish and place in the freezer for 15 minutes to chill. Dock the bottom of the crust with a fork and bake for 12 to 15 minutes, or until golden brown.

2 Whisk the egg yolks in a small bowl and set aside.

3 In a medium saucepan, combine the 2/3 cup sugar, flour, 2 cups heavy cream, coconut cream, dried strawberries, and lemon zest over low heat. Stir continuously until the mixture starts to bubble up on the sides of the pan, but don't allow mixture to boil.

4 Pour one-quarter of the hot mixture into the egg yolks, stirring continuously in order to temper the egg yolks. Pour the egg yolk mixture back into the saucepan and whisk to combine.

continued

5 Continue stirring until the mixture begins to thicken, 3 to 5 additional minutes. Remove from the heat and add the shredded coconut. Pour the filling into the baked piecrust, cover with plastic wrap, and let set in the refrigerator for 4 hours until set.

6 Once set, prepare the colored whipped cream topping. Pour the 4 cups heavy cream and 3 table-spoons sugar into a large mixing bowl and beat on medium-high for about 5 minutes, or until it has soft peaks.

7 Remove one-half of the whipped cream from the mixing bowl and set aside. Tint remaining whipped cream in the mixing bowl red-orange by adding two dabs of red and one dab of orange food coloring and continue to whip a couple more minutes until it has stiff peaks. Cover with plastic wrap and put into the fridge. Divide the remaining whipped cream into two bowls, with two-thirds in one bowl, and one-third in another. The bowl with the remaining two-thirds whipped cream is to be colored blue, and the one-third whipped cream colored green. Do this by using a toothpick or a chopstick to add the color and hand whip into the whipped cream with a whisk. Put in two separate zip-top bags and put in the fridge until ready to use.

8 Remove the pie from the refrigerator. Spread the red-orange tinted whipped cream over the entire top of the pie. Cut the corner of each zip-top bag and pipe small blue mounds all the way around the pie, with one single large green mound of whipped cream in the middle.

ROYAL TARTS

(Inspired by *Adventure Time*)

Make way for the Royal Tart Toter! Fresh strawberries combined with strawberry gelatin create the most perfectly sweet tart—Princess Bubblegum would be proud. Obviously, this makes a fantastic dessert for one, but you could also make these for your very own Royal Back-Rubbing Ceremony. We won't make you transport these across the Bad Lands. Just make sure you are the one getting the back rubbing, dude!

Prep Time: 3 hours 35 minutes
Total Time: 4 hours
Serves: 6 Candy Kingdom citizens

Ingredients

1 recipe Tart Crust (page 175) or refrigerated ready-made piecrust

Strawberry Glaze

2½ cups fresh strawberries, plus 3 whole strawberries

1 cup granulated sugar

2 tablespoons corn syrup

2½ tablespoons cornstarch

2 tablespoons strawberry gelatin

Instructions

1 Preheat the oven to 350°F.

2 Prepare the Tart Crust recipe according to the instructions on page 175 or if using a ready-made piecrust, remove the piecrust dough from the fridge. After the dough has reached room temperature, divide the dough into six pieces. On a floured surface, roll each piece out into a flat disk a little larger than a mini tart pan.

3 Shape the dough carefully into six mini tart pans, using a paring knife to cut around the top of the pan to even it out if necessary. Place all six on a baking sheet and dock each mini tart with a fork. Put back into the freezer for 20 minutes before baking.

4 Bake the tart crusts for 20 minutes, until golden brown. Rotate the tarts halfway through baking in the oven to get an even bake. Let the tarts cool completely.

continued

5 Prepare the glaze: Puree the fresh strawberries in a food processor or blender.

6 In a medium saucepan over low heat, combine the sugar, corn syrup, and cornstarch with ¾ cup water.

7 Add the pureed strawberries and bring to boil, stirring consistently until thickened, 3 to 5 minutes.

8 Remove from the heat and stir in the strawberry gelatin.

9 Strain the strawberry glaze through a sieve to remove seeds and residual lumps of gelatin or cornstarch.

10 Pour the mixture into the prepared mini tarts and put in refrigerator to cool for at least 2 hours.

11 Cut the three whole strawberries in half and place in the middle of each tart before serving.

LEMON CAKES

(Inspired by *Game of Thrones*)

Dealing with the White Walkers, wildling raids, and constant threat of kinslaying can definitely leave even the most seasoned winter warrior hankering for a sweet treat. Lemon cakes are Sansa's favorite, and we can see why. Like our Queen in the North, these mini lemon soufflé cakes are delicate on the outside, but hide a memorable tart flavor on the inside. This recipe produces fairly bite-sized portions, perfect for a midafternoon tea or even a meeting with the matriarch of the Tyrells to plan the poisoning of your royal husband. Or, you know, whatever you like to do!

Prep Time: 30 minutes
Cook time: 60 minutes
Serves: 6 summer children

Ingredients

½ cup granulated sugar

3 tablespoons plus 1 teaspoon all-purpose flour

⅛ teaspoon salt

2 large eggs, separated

⅔ cup buttermilk

2½ tablespoons fresh lemon juice

Zest of 1½ lemons

1 teaspoon vanilla extract

Confectioners' sugar for dusting

3 lemons for garnish

Instructions

1 Preheat the oven to 300°F. Butter a 6-cup muffin tin. Cut six circles out of parchment paper (the size of the bottom of each cup) and place in the middle of each buttered cup.

2 In a medium bowl, sift together the sugar, flour, and salt and set aside.

3 Beat the 2 egg whites with a mixer until you achieve soft peaks. Set aside.

4 Whisk together the buttermilk, lemon juice, lemon zest, vanilla extract, and egg yolks in a large bowl. Slowly whisk in the flour mixture and then fold in the egg whites until no white remains.

5 Divide the batter among the muffin wells. Prepare a water bath by placing the muffin tin in an oblong cake pan and fill it with boiling water to right underneath the top of the muffin tin. Cover the entire tin with aluminum foil.

continued

6 Bake for 25 minutes and uncover. Bake for an additional 15 to 20 minutes, until the cakes are golden brown. Remove from the water bath and let cool for at least 15 minutes before unmolding.

7 Use a knife to loosen each cake from the muffin tin. Flip over onto a plate or serving dish. Dust confectioners' sugar with a sifter or a fine metal strainer.

8 Using a sharp paring knife or vegetable peeler, start at the top of each lemon and cutting the yellow rind only, do not include the white part of the peel, pare around each lemon in a 1/2-inch-wide continuous strip, making the cuts jagged and wavy as your knife is cutting. Repeat with other lemons. Coil the lemon peel strips in a circle, skin side out, as tightly as possible without breaking the strip to create lemon roses. Cut the lemon roses in the middle of the lemon rind to create six mini roses. Garnish each cake with a rose.

SEA SALT ICE CREAM

(Inspired by *Kingdom Hearts*)

We've been trying to decipher the story of the Kingdom Hearts series for almost 20 years now, and honestly we just get more confused the more we play. The one thing we know for sure are the two most important tenets of the story—light and friendship. Sea salt ice cream? Well, that's just a bonus. You don't have to have an in with Scrooge McDuck OR an ice cream maker to pull off this sweet and salty treat. This recipe has been key to our channel, but this new and improved version uses butterfly pea powder to color the custard. It's completely natural and we think it's an even closer match to the animated pop in the game. Save yourself a trip to Twilight Town and synthesize this treat from scratch, kupo!

Prep Time: 30 minutes
Total Time: 4 hours 30 minutes
Serves: 8 Organization XIII members

Ingredients

2 eggs, separated
⅓ cup granulated sugar
2 cups milk
1 teaspoon butterfly pea powder
½ teaspoon vanilla extract
⅓ teaspoon sea salt, plus more for garnish
1 cup heavy cream

Instructions

1 Beat the egg whites in a large bowl to stiff peaks by hand or with a mixer. Be sure not to overwhip.

2 In a medium bowl, add the sugar to the egg yolks. Whisk until light yellow and fluffy.

3 In a medium saucepan, heat the milk on low-medium heat until it starts to simmer. Temper the egg mixture with one-quarter of the hot milk, then pour the egg yolks back into the saucepan, whisking continuously so that the egg yolks don't scramble.

4 Stir until simmering. Remove from the heat. Add the butterfly pea powder and vanilla extract.

continued

5 Pour the milk mixture into a large mixing bowl and whisk in the egg whites. Add ½ teaspoon of the sea salt.

6 Pop the bowl into the fridge to cool for 15 minutes. Once cooled, whisk in the heavy cream.

7 Pour the mixture into popsicle molds and put into the freezer for at least 4 hours. Take the ice pops out of the molds when ready to serve and sprinkle with sea salt.

Cheat Code: You're the wielder of this recipe, so if gel food coloring is more your style, then feel free to use that as an alternative to butterfly pea powder.

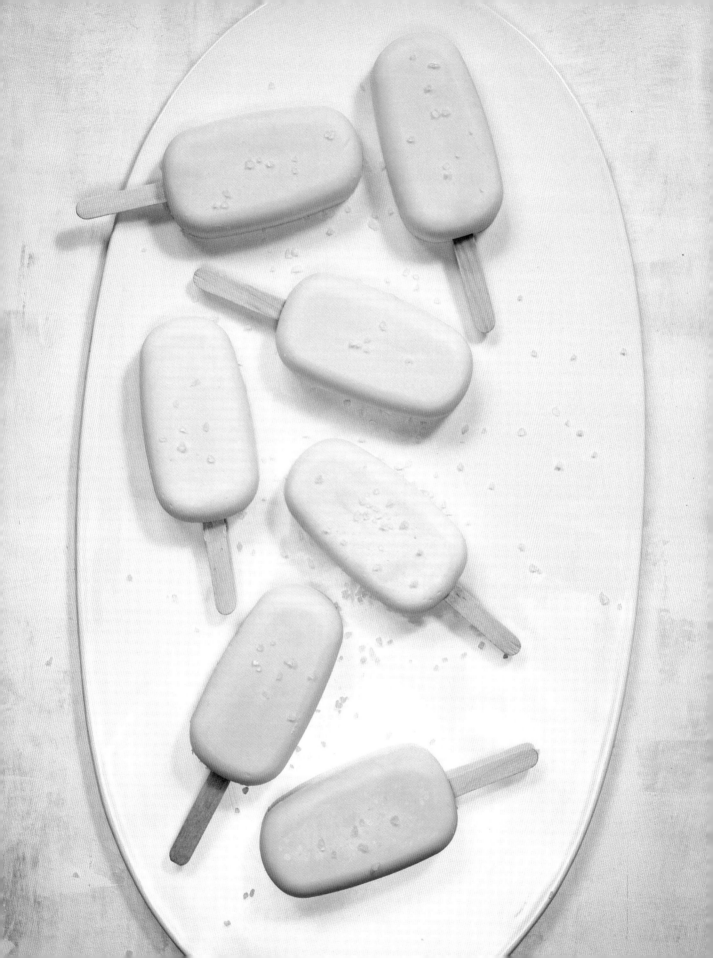

HOMEMADE POKÉ BLOCKS

(Inspired by *Pokémon*)

Like everything else in Pokémon, *Poké Blocks are awesome because they're just so darn cute! These mini petit four cakes are fully customizable in any flavor and color combination you want. While there are no Pokémon in real life to feed these to, not yet anyway, you can definitely share them with friends and colleagues to buff up the most important statistic of all—friendship!*

Prep Time: 1 hour 30 minutes
Total Time: 1 hour 50 minutes
Serves: 40 Pokémon (or their trainers)

Ingredients

Sheet Cake

½ pound (2 sticks) unsalted butter, at room
    temperature
1½ cups granulated sugar
3 large eggs
1 teaspoon vanilla extract
2¼ cups all-purpose flour
½ teaspoon baking powder
¼ teaspoon sea salt
¾ cup milk
½ recipe Swiss Meringue Buttercream recipe (see
    page 179)

Filling

½ cup jam (raspberry, blueberry, orange marmalade,
    lemon curd, or mint jam are good variations if you
    want to flavor your Blocks to coordinate with the
    colors)

Poured Fondant Icing

6 cups confectioners' sugar
2 tablespoons corn syrup, light
½ teaspoon almond extract
¾ cup white chocolate chips
Gel food coloring (pink, blue, yellow, orange)
a skewer

continued

Instructions

1 Preheat the oven to 350°F. Grease and flour a 13-by-18-inch half-sheet pan and line with parchment paper.

2 Cream the butter and sugar in a large bowl or the bowl of a stand mixer until light and fluffy, 4 to 5 minutes. Gradually add the eggs, scraping well after they are incorporated. Add the vanilla and mix to combine.

3 In a medium bowl, mix the flour, baking powder, and salt. Add the dry ingredients to the mixer and mix on low speed to combine. Add the milk and keep mixing until combined.

4 Pour the batter into the prepared pan and bake 20 to 25 minutes. Insert a toothpick to check if done. If the toothpick comes out clean, it's finished. Cool the cake to room temperature.

5 While the cake is baking, prepare half of the Swiss Meringue Buttercream frosting recipe, according to the instructions on page 179.

6 When the cake is cooled, cut the cake down the middle to make two even halves. Cut each half into four even strip-type layers. This should give you four top and bottom layers. Evenly spread a heavy layer of jam on each strip of cake and top with a different strip of cake. (If you are coordinating the flavors to the color of Block, make sure each strip gets a different flavor of jam.)

7 Frost the rest of the cakes with the buttercream frosting, making the tops and sides as smooth as possible. Freeze the cakes for at least 45 minutes, as cutting a cooled cake is easier than a room temperature one.

8 Prepare the Poured Fondant Icing while the cakes are cooling. Fill a medium saucepan with 1 cup water and bring to a simmer on low heat. Whisk together the confectioners' sugar, corn syrup, and almond extract with $2/3$ cup of water in a large heat-safe mixing bowl to combine. Place the bowl over the top of the pot of simmering water to create a double boiler. Continue to stir frequently until mixture becomes smooth and homogenous.

9 Pour in the white chocolate chips and continue to stir until completely melted. The mixture should be fluid, but not too warm, keeping the temperature under 100°F.

10 Prepare a cooling rack on top of cans the same size (e.g., two cola cans or two cans of peas) with parchment underneath. Set aside.

11 Equally divide the poured fondant between four bowls and tint each bowl accordingly with the gel food coloring.

12 Pull the cakes out of the freezer and cut into small squares (about 1 to 1¼ inches). You want them to be as similar in size as possible, so using a ruler is also a good idea. Time is of the essence here, as working with frozen cake makes for the best possible outcome. Feel free to put them back into the freezer to reset if this process takes longer than expected.

13 Stick a skewer into the bottom of a square, and then dip the cake square into one of the bowls of poured fondant. Swirl the square into the mixture to completely coat, then pull it out of the mixture, letting the excess drip off the sides. Drop the skewer into one of the squares of the cooling rack and slide out the skewer for the petit four to set.

14 Repeat step 13 to create the next color in the sequence of Blocks until all cake squares are evenly coated in the different colors.

COOKIE CAT

(Inspired by *Steven Universe*)

Cookie Cat—"It's a cat for your tummy!" More important, it's an ice cream sandwich that makes us nostalgic for hot summer nights and rushing into the street, dollars in hand, when we heard the iconic tunes coming from the neighborhood ice cream truck. This cookie is soft enough to melt in your mouth, but it's dense enough to handle a serious glob of ice cream. It's surprisingly fun to make ice cream sandwiches from scratch, and take it from us, this recipe is a gem.

Prep Time: 1 hour 30 minutes
Total Time: 2 hours
Serves: 8 to 10 Crystal Gems

Ingredients

1 cup all-purpose flour

½ cup dark Dutch process cocoa powder

¼ teaspoon salt

½ cup granulated sugar

8 tablespoons (1 stick) unsalted butter, softened

1 large egg

1 teaspoon vanilla extract

½ teaspoon almond extract

½ gallon vanilla ice cream

½ gallon strawberry ice cream

Instructions

1 Preheat the oven to 325°F.

2 In a medium bowl, sift together the flour, cocoa, and salt and set aside.

3 Cream the sugar and butter in a large bowl or the bowl of a stand mixer until light and fluffy. Add the egg and extracts and mix to incorporate. Reduce the speed to low and slowly add in the dry ingredients. Beat until a firm dough forms. Divide into two disks, wrap in plastic wrap, and chill in the refrigerator for 20 minutes.

4 For the cookie cutters, use a thin strip of hanger strap from your local hardware store. Draw your cookie cat design on a piece of parchment paper. Shape the strip of hanger strap around the design to create a cat-shaped cookie cutter. Use the hard edge of a book or box to make cleaner folds for the cookie cutter. Use a pencil or pen when going around the ears or doing any small curved edges. When you've finished, trim the excess metal and tape off your cookie cutter to stay in place.

continued

5 For the ice cream, line a 10-by-13-inch baking sheet with parchment paper. Cut to fit the size of the pan horizontally and let the edges of the parchment hang off vertically. First, spread the vanilla ice cream in a 2½-inch row the length of 13 inches. Cut a strip of parchment to line the outside of the vanilla strip, making a barrier of sorts. Make it as straight as possible and put in the freezer to refreeze for at least 15 minutes. Once refrozen, remove the sheet from the freezer, remove the parchment strip, and add an equal row of strawberry ice cream next to the vanilla strip. Make another parchment divider and put the sheet back in freezer for 15 minutes. Repeat this process again with the vanilla and the strawberry until the pan is filled up with two alternating rows of vanilla and strawberry. Cover with plastic wrap and pop back in the freezer and refreeze.

6 Roll out the cookie dough about ¼ of an inch thick between two pieces of parchment paper and put back into fridge to chill for 10 more minutes (the dough is easiest to use while cold). Use the cutter to cut the dough into Cookie Cats. Repeat with excess dough to make more cookie cats. Use the small round cutter or the bottom of a metal piping tip to make eyes in half of the cats you cut out. Chill the dough in the freezer for 10 minutes, then bake for 12 to 14 minutes and let cool completely.

7 Remove the baking sheet of ice cream from the freezer. Dip the cookie cutter in a bowl of hot water before cutting into the ice cream to make a smoother cut. Place the Cookie Cat cutter in between one row of vanilla and strawberry to get a half vanilla, half strawberry cookie cat. Put the ice cream cutout onto the bottom cookie of a Cookie Cat, and top with the cookie with the eyes cut out. Place in freezer to refreeze as an ice cream sandwich.

⚡ *Cheat Code:* You can use regular cocoa powder as a substitute if you have it lying around, but dark or Dutch process cocoa powder will make your batter darker in color and more akin to the fictional Cookie Cat.

MINI BLACK FOREST CAKES

(Inspired by *Portal*)

*Although the cake in **Portal** is never something you get to enjoy in game, take comfort knowing that the version we've created is anything but a lie. We took the spirit of Black Forest cake and made it into a personal-sized dessert, so now everyone at your party can get a mini cake to themselves! And who wouldn't want to devour a cake that's been coated in chocolate ganache, chocolate shards, and hides a cherry creme filling inside. Just don't tell GLaDOS . . . seriously.*

Prep Time: 1 hour
Total Time: 1 hour 15 minutes
Makes: 7 or 8 mini black forest cakes

Ingredients

Devil's Food Cake recipe (page 177)
One 15-ounce can dark sweet cherries in heavy syrup
1 tablespoon cherry liqueur (optional)
One to two 4-ounce bars semisweet chocolate
Maraschino cherries for garnish

Whipped Cream

½ cup heavy cream
1 tablespoon granulated sugar
½ teaspoon vanilla extract

Chocolate Ganache

1 cup heavy cream
½ cup semisweet chocolate chips

Instructions

1 Preheat the oven to 350°F. Line a 9-by-13-inch baking pan with parchment paper and grease with oil. Make the Devil's Food Cake recipe according to the instructions on page 177 and pour it into the prepared pan. Bake for 12 to 15 minutes, until a toothpick comes out clean. Set aside and let cool to room temperature.

2 Once the cake is cool, use a 3-inch round cookie cutter to cut out 14 to 16 circles of cake. Cut each circle in half. Scoop out a divot in each half with a teaspoon. Set aside.

3 Drain the sweet dark cherries, reserving ¼ cup of heavy syrup. If adding cherry liqueur, simmer with the heavy syrup in a small saucepan until the liquid has reduced by one-quarter, about 15 minutes. Brush the cherry syrup over the bottom layer of each cake. There will be some syrup left over; set it aside.

4 Dice the dark sweet cherries. Set aside.

continued

5 Using a cheese grater, grate the semisweet chocolate bars into chocolate shavings into a small bowl and set aside.

6 For the whipping cream, combine ½ cup heavy cream, sugar, and vanilla extract and in the mixing bowl of a stand mixer, beat on medium-high until it forms medium peaks, about 5 minutes.

7 To make the ganache, heat 1 cup heavy cream in a saucepan until it begins to simmer. Pour it over the chocolate chips in a heat-safe bowl and let sit for 2 minutes before stirring to combine. Let sit at room temperature while assembling the mini cakes.

8 To assemble the mini cakes, start with a teaspoon of whipped cream in the divot, add some diced cherries, and a drizzle of cherry syrup. Brush more cherry syrup on the cake around the divot and place the other half on top to close the mini cake. Repeat until all the mini cakes are filled.

9 Place the mini cakes on a drying rack on top of a baking sheet, and using a ladle, pour the cooled ganache over them. Smooth with an offset spatula or a butter knife. Let set for 5 minutes, and then press chocolate shavings into the side and sprinkle on the top. Repeat until all mini cakes are covered in ganache and shavings.

10 Pipe a dollop of whipped cream on top, and place a maraschino cherry in the middle.

⚡ *Cheat Code:* If you are in a time crunch, just buy a box of devil's food cake instead of making it from scratch.

DIREWOLF SHORTBREAD

(Inspired by *Game of Thrones*)

The direwolf is the house sigil of the Starks in Game of Thrones, *and this mythical creature plays a major part throughout the story by accompanying the children of this noble house through thick and thin. We get to see the direwolf immortalized in baked form by Hot Pie, so we decided to create a blood orange and rosemary shortbread instead of a typical bread. These sweet and savory elements mixed together give this direwolf layers of complexity and help fuel that inner fire an adventurer needs as Winter approaches the Seven Kingdoms.*

Prep Time: 30 minutes
Total Time: 50 minutes
Serves: 4 Stark children

Ingredients

2¼ cups whole wheat flour

1 teaspoon salt

2 teaspoons finely chopped fresh rosemary

½ cup granulated sugar

3 tablespoons blood orange juice

Zest of 2 blood oranges, finely grated

Zest of 1 lemon, finely grated

½ pound (2 sticks) unsalted butter

1 teaspoon vanilla extract

Instructions

1 Preheat the oven to 350°F. Line two baking sheets with parchment paper.

2 In a medium bowl, whisk the flour, salt, and rosemary together.

3 In the bowl of a stand mixer, whisk the sugar, blood orange juice, and both citrus zests until combined.

4 Add the butter and beat until well combined. Add the vanilla extract. Slowly add the dry ingredients and mix until combined.

5 Drop the dough onto a floured surface. You may need to turn the dough a couple of times by hand in case the ingredients weren't fully incorporated by the mixer.

6 Roll out the dough to about ½ inch thick.

continued

7 Trace a direwolf template on a piece of parchment paper and cut out with kitchen shears to create a stencil.

8 Lie the stencil on top of the dough and cut around it with a knife. Place the direwolf-shaped shortbreads onto the parchment-lined baking sheet. Score the dough with a knife, and use a fork to give the shortbread the wolf-like texture. Repeat 6 to 8 times until all the dough is cut out.

9 Bake for 20 minutes, or until the edges of the direwolf are golden brown.

AMBROSIA SQUARES

(Inspired by the Percy Jackson series)

When Percy Jackson gets to taste the mythical ambrosia, the food of the gods, he compares the taste to his mom's freshly baked chocolate chip cookies. Heavenly! So, when creating a dessert worthy of Mount Olympus, we found inspiration in our moms's cookie recipes. Ooey, gooey, and oh so shareable, you might find yourself making these for every party, bake sale, and family reunion. These chocolate chip cookie bars also tip their hat to traditional American ambrosia salad (you know, that fluffy pink fruit goo from the '50s) with coconut oil and shredded coconut. It's the best of both worlds—well, except maybe the underworld.

Prep Time: 25 minutes
Total Time: 45 minutes
Serves: 9 deities of Olympus

Ingredients

2 cups all-purpose flour

1 teaspoon baking powder

½ teaspoon sea salt, plus more for garnish

1 cup dark brown sugar

½ cup coconut oil, melted then cooled

1 large egg

1 egg yolk

1 tablespoon vanilla extract

1 cup dark chocolate chips

½ cup sweetened shredded coconut

Instructions

1 Preheat the oven to 350°F. Line an 8-inch square baking pan with parchment paper.

2 Mix the flour, baking powder, and salt in a large bowl. In a separate medium bowl, mix the brown sugar and coconut oil together. Once combined, add the egg and egg yolk. Stir in the vanilla.

3 Combine the wet ingredients with the dry ingredients. Fold in the chocolate chips and shredded coconut.

4 Spread the batter evenly in the prepared pan and bake for 20 minutes. Sprinkle with sea salt while still warm.

DOUBLE-GLAZED APPLE FRITTERS

(Inspired by Regular Show)

We could sit here and describe what this recipe is, or you could just read the name of the recipe over and over again. Double. Glazed. Apple. Fritters. This is it. The full flavor profile. Their taste? Magic. Their effect? A sugar rush second to none. Rigby and Mordecai approved, these apple fritters are just what you need to turn any occasion into the ultimate party.

Prep Time: 10 minutes
Total Time: 20 minutes
Serves: 24 party animals

Ingredients

3 Granny Smith apples
2 teaspoons lemon juice
1 cup all-purpose flour
2 tablespoons granulated sugar
2 teaspoons baking powder
½ teaspoon cinnamon
¼ teaspoon nutmeg
½ teaspoon salt
2 large eggs, room temperature
⅔ cup milk
1 tablespoon vegetable oil
Canola oil, for frying

Glaze

2 cups confectioners' sugar
½ teaspoon vanilla extract

Instructions

1 Peel, core, and dice the apples into tiny cubes. Toss in the lemon juice and set aside.

2 In a medium bowl, stir together the flour, sugar, baking powder, cinnamon, nutmeg, and salt.

3 In a separate large bowl, combine the eggs, milk, and oil and stir until combined. Pour the flour mixture in gradually and whisk until combined.

4 Fold in the apples and stir until the apples are coated.

5 Heat the canola oil in a medium saucepan over medium heat to 375°F using a candy thermometer. Drop an ice cream scoop full of batter into the oil and let it fry until golden brown, about 3 to 5 minutes. Be sure both sides are cooked to golden brown. Pierce the fritter to the center to check for doneness. If not done, fry 1 to 2 minutes longer. Transfer to a paper towel-lined plate to cool. Repeat with the remaining batter.

continued

6 Prepare the glaze by combining the confectioners' sugar and vanilla extract and gradually pouring 1/3 cup of water into a medium bowl and stirring until completely combined. The glaze should be smooth, so add the water slowly and mix it until pourable consistency is obtained. It's okay if you don't use all the water; the consistency is what's important.

7 Dip the fritters into the glaze and swirl around until completely coated. Let set on a cooling rack sitting atop a baking sheet. Once all the fritters are dipped, take the remaining glaze and drizzle over the fritters to make them double glazed.

SQUIRRELMUM'S BLACKBERRY AND APPLE CAKE

(Inspired by the Redwall series)

One of Jimmy's first introductions to fantastical foods (and the inspiration for our online show) was the Redwall series by Brian Jacques. Just reading the incredibly detailed descriptions of these amazing foods and desserts was more than enough to get our brains whirring on how to bring these recipes to real life. With a succulent caramel sauce drizzle, this blackberry and apple cake is a showstopper at the table and an appetite buster in the belly.

Prep Time: 30 minutes
Total Time: 1 hour 30 minutes
Serves: 12 squirrels

Ingredients

2 cups granulated sugar

½ cup canola oil

2 large eggs

2 egg yolks

1 teaspoon vanilla extract

¼ cup sour cream

2½ cups all-purpose flour

3 teaspoons baking powder

1 teaspoon salt

1 cup buttermilk

1 to 2 Granny Smith apples

2 cups blackberries

Caramel Sauce

1 cup granulated sugar

½ cup heavy cream

1 teaspoon vanilla extract

1 tablespoon sea salt

Instructions

1 Preheat the oven to 350°F. Line a 10-inch spring-form pan with a circle of parchment paper and set aside.

2 Combine the 2 cups sugar, oil, eggs, egg yolks, and vanilla extract in a large mixing bowl or the bowl of a stand mixer and mix until well combined. Mix in the sour cream and beat until smooth.

3 Combine the flour, baking powder, and 1 teaspoon salt. Add the dry ingredients and the buttermilk alternately to the sugar-oil-egg mixture until all the ingredients are fully incorporated.

4 Core and cut the apples into very thin slices either using a knife or a mandolin. Cut the apple slices in half.

5 Layer the fruit by outlining the pan with the blackberries. Inside the row of blackberries, create a row of apples overlapping each other, then repeat

continued

alternating rows until the entire bottom of the pan is covered with fruit.

6 Pour the cake batter over the fruit and bake on a baking sheet.

7 Bake for 45 minutes to 1 hour, until a toothpick comes out clean of crumbs. Let cool completely.

8 Make the caramel sauce while the cake is cooling. Add ⅓ cup of water and the 1 cup sugar to a medium saucepan over medium heat and stir occasionally until it comes to a boil. Once it starts to boil, stop stirring. (The continuation of stirring at this point in the process could lead to crystallization.) Once the mixture becomes a nice, golden brown in color (after about 8 to 10 minutes undisturbed), pull the pan from the heat. While stirring continuously, add the heavy cream, vanilla extract, and sea salt.

9 Open the springform and flip the cake onto a serving tray. Drizzle the caramel sauce over the top of the cake and serve!

#13 Pizza Gyoza (TMNT)

2 cloves of garlic   1/3 cup romano cheese
1 cup italian sausage   1/2 cup parmesan
1/2 cup pepperoni   1 tsp fennel
1/2 cup onion, minced   3 tbsp basil

Sift your flour into a bowl and add salt. Slowly add

#42 Calzo

2 cups

2 c

Charcuterie Plate from Edward Scissorhands

SANTHA BLUE MILK FROM STAR

Roald Dahl's "The Twits" Calzone for Two

1 package of puff pastry
1 tbsp olive oil
4 tbsp onion, diced
1 tbsp garlic, sliced
2 cloves of garlic, diced
4 stalks of celery, diced

In
gar
is b
from
chil
and pep

e Bears)

1/2 tsp pepper

1 cup mozzarella

2 tbsp basil

2 cloves garlic

to

oval

ju cut out.

for 15.

y floured surface, divide refrigerated

ugh) roll out each piece into a circle about the

thickness of a dry lasagna noodle.

Ro

cut it i

cutter to make

Chill in freezer for

Bacon Pancakes from

1 ½ cups all-purpose

2 tablespoons sugar

1 tablespoon baking

1/2 teaspoon of ba

Add a square of bu

ladle full of batt

a large circle pancak

middle in the shape o

brown. To serve, sta

plate and top with the rem

pancake mouth down first, then his eyes

pancake mouth down to make a small line

leftover melted dark chocolate to create a smile.

the inside of his pancake mouth to create a smile.

a toothpick.

salt. Slowly add

stirring continously. Add

at a time, if dough seems too

gh into a ball and place in a bowl.

m

dry

Baking
Essentials

SIMPLE SYRUP

Makes: 1½ cups

Ingredients

1 cup water
1 cup granulated sugar

Instructions

1 Pour the water and sugar in a small saucepan over medium heat and stir until the sugar is dissolved. The liquid will be clear.

2 It's best to store in an airtight container in the fridge until use.

BUTTERFLY PEA SIMPLE SYRUP

Makes: 2 cups

Ingredients

2 cups water
1 teaspoon butterfly pea powder
½ cup granulated sugar

Instructions

1 In a saucepan, combine the water with sugar over medium heat. Stir in the butterfly pea powder and bring to a simmer. Remove from the heat and let cool.

2 It's best to store in an airtight container in the fridge until use.

PIECRUST (PÂTE BRISÉE)

Makes: 1 piecrust

Ingredients

2½ cups all-purpose flour

1 teaspoon salt

1 teaspoon granulated sugar

½ pound (2 sticks) unsalted butter, chilled

Instructions

1 Add the flour, salt, and sugar into a large mixing bowl. Add the butter and, using a fork or a pastry cutter, mix into the flour until the mixture resembles coarse crumbs.

2 Knead the dough (with your hands or a stand mixer) and add 1 tablespoon of cold water at a time until a smooth dough forms. (Be careful not to add too much water or overwork!) Divide the dough into two, form disks, wrap in plastic wrap, and put in the fridge to chill for at least 2 hours before using.

TART CRUST (PÂTE SUCRÉE)

Makes: 1 crust

Ingredients

½ pound (2 sticks) unsalted butter

2 tablespoons granulated sugar

2½ cups all-purpose flour

2 large egg yolks

¼ cup ice water, plus more if necessary

Instructions

1 In the bowl of a food processor, combine the butter and sugar. Add the flour and pulse until the mixture resembles sand, about 10 to 15 seconds.

2 Add the egg yolks and cold water and process until the mixture forms a dough. Add more water by the teaspoon if dough is too crumbly.

3 Divide the dough into two equal balls. Flatten each ball into a disk, wrap in plastic wrap, and let chill in the refrigerator for at least 1 hour.

VANILLA CAKE

Makes: One 8-inch double layer cake

Ingredients

1¾ cups granulated sugar

½ pound (2 sticks) unsalted butter

3 large eggs

2 teaspoons vanilla extract

2 cups all-purpose flour

2¼ teaspoons baking powder

½ teaspoon salt

1 cup milk

Instructions

1 Preheat the oven to 350°F. Grease and line two 8-inch round cake pans with parchment paper.

2 In a medium bowl, cream together the sugar and butter.

3 Beat in the eggs, one at a time, then stir in the vanilla.

4 In a medium bowl, combine the flour, baking powder, and salt. Add slowly into the creamed mixture and mix until combined.

5 Stir in the milk until the batter is smooth. Pour the batter into the pans and bake for 20 to 25 minutes, until a toothpick comes out clean.

VANILLA CUPCAKES

Makes: 12 cupcakes

Ingredients

1 cup granulated sugar

8 tablespoons (1 stick) unsalted butter

2 large eggs

2 teaspoons vanilla extract

1½ cups all-purpose flour

2 teaspoons baking powder

½ teaspoon salt

½ cup milk

Instructions

1 Preheat the oven to 350°F. Line a 12-cup muffin tin with paper liners.

2 In a medium bowl or the bowl of a stand mixer, cream together the sugar and butter.

3 Beat in the eggs, one at a time, then stir in the vanilla.

4 In a medium bowl, combine the flour, baking powder, and salt. Add slowly into the creamed mixture and mix until combined.

5 Stir in the milk until the batter is smooth. Pour or spoon the batter into the liners.

6 Bake for 15 to 17 minutes, or until a toothpick comes out clean.

⚡ *Cheat Code:* You can add different extracts to create different flavored cupcakes.

DEVIL'S FOOD CAKE

Makes: Two 8-inch layers

Ingredients

½ pound (2 sticks) unsalted butter, plus some for greasing pan

¾ cup cocoa powder, plus more for dusting pan

2 cups all-purpose flour

1 teaspoon salt

1 teaspoon baking powder

2 teaspoons baking soda

2 cups granulated sugar

1 cup brewed coffee

1 cup canola oil

1 cup buttermilk

2 large eggs

1 teaspoon vanilla extract

Instructions

1 Line two 8-inch cake pans with a circle of parchment paper in each. Grease both pans with butter and dust them with cocoa powder.

2 Whisk together the flour, salt, baking powder, baking soda, and cocoa powder in a large bowl.

3 Cream the butter and sugar in the bowl of a stand mixer. Add the coffee, oil, buttermilk, eggs, and vanilla. Mix in the dry ingredients.

4 Pour the batter into the prepared round cake pans and bake for 30 to 40 minutes, until a toothpick comes out clean.

5 Let cool in pans until warm and then remove from pans by loosening the edges with a knife or offset spatula.

WHIPPED CREAM

Makes: 2 cups

Ingredients

1 cup heavy cream

2 tablespoons granulated sugar

½ teaspoon vanilla extract

Instructions

1 Add the cream, sugar, and vanilla to a large bowl or the bowl of a stand mixer. Using a whisk or whisk attachment, beat until thickened to desired consistency.

AMERICAN BUTTER-CREAM

Makes: 5 cups

Ingredients

1 pound (4 sticks) unsalted butter
8 cups confectioners' sugar, plus more if needed
2 tablespoons heavy cream, plus more if needed
½ teaspoon salt
1 teaspoon vanilla extract

Instructions

1 Beat the butter in the bowl of a stand mixer until the butter is creamy.

2 Turn the mixer to low and slowly add the confectioners' sugar, intermittently adding the heavy cream, until fully incorporated. Add the vanilla and salt.

3 If frosting is too thick, add more heavy cream by the tablespoon. If too thin, add more sugar by ½ cup at a time.

CREAM CHEESE BUTTER-CREAM

Makes: 5 cups

Ingredients

Two 8-ounce packages cream cheese
½ pound (2 sticks) unsalted butter
8 cups confectioners' sugar
2 teaspoons vanilla extract
2 tablespoons heavy cream, plus more if necessary

Instructions

1 Place the cream cheese and butter in the bowl of a stand mixer and beat until creamy.

2 Turn the mixer to low, slowly add the confectioners' sugar, scraping down the sides of the bowl with a spatula when necessary.

3 Add the vanilla and heavy cream. Add more heavy cream by the tablespoon to obtain a nice, smooth consistency if necessary.

SWISS MERINGUE BUTTER-CREAM

Makes: 6 cups

Ingredients

6 large egg whites
1½ cups granulated sugar
Pinch of salt
1 pound (4 sticks) unsalted butter, softened
2 teaspoons vanilla extract

Instructions

1 Combine the egg whites, sugar, and salt in a heat-safe bowl (or the bowl of a stand mixer) above a saucepan of simmering water. Stir constantly until the sugar has completely dissolved, or until the egg white mixture reaches 160°F.

2 Transfer the egg white mixture to a stand mixer with the whisk attachment, start whisking on low but gradually increase to medium-high speed until your meringue reaches stiff peaks. They should be glossy and smooth. Mix for about 10 minutes. The meringue should be cooled before you start adding the butter.

3 Turn the mixer back to low and add the butter 1 tablespoon at a time. Butter should be incorporated each time before new addition. Once the butter is completely incorporated, add the vanilla extract. At this point, the mixture may look curdled and soupy. Turn the mixer on medium-high and beat until whipped and fluffy, about 7 to 10 minutes.

CHOCOLATE GANACHE

Makes: 1½ cups

Ingredients

1 cup heavy cream
½ cup semisweet chocolate chips

Instructions

1 Heat the heavy cream in a small saucepan over medium heat until it begins to simmer. Pour over the chocolate in a heat-safe bowl and let sit for 2 minutes before stirring to combine.

EASY PIZZA DOUGH

Makes: 1 pizza crust

Ingredients

1 teaspoon granulated sugar

2¼ teaspoons dry active yeast

2 teaspoons olive oil, plus additional for the bowl

2 cups all-purpose flour, additional for dusting

¾ teaspoon salt

½ teaspoon garlic powder

Instructions

1. Add ¾ cup of warm water to a large bowl or the bowl of a stand mixer. Stir in the sugar and yeast. Let sit for 5 minutes until frothy.

2. Add the oil and stir well.

3. Add 1 cup of the flour, salt, and garlic powder and mix. Continue to add flour gradually until the mixture balls up, pulling away from the sides of the bowl. The dough should still be slightly sticky but able to be handled.

4. Generously grease a separate large bowl with olive oil. Form the dough into a round ball and drop it into the greased bowl. Roll the dough around the bowl until it is coated with olive oil, cover with plastic wrap, and let rise in a warm place for 30 minutes, or until doubled in size.

5. Once the dough has risen, deflate it with a couple of squeezes from your fingers, transfer to a lightly floured surface, and knead for a couple of minutes until smooth.

6. Roll out the pizza dough with a rolling pin. Don't forget to dock your pizza crust with a fork to keep it from puffing up while baking.

Acknowledgments

Ashley: I'd like to thank my parents. To my mom for instilling in me the concepts of diligence and passion and for the lesson of faith that anything I put my mind to would be mine. For cultivating and nourishing a daughter with a creative mind and spirit, and always being the most positive, brightest light in my world for the 13 years that she was in it. And to my dad, who bestowed upon me his strong-willed mentality and unwavering work ethic. He was the true chef of the family. His tough love encouraged me to always be better, especially in the kitchen, and I will continue to carry that with me as I further my culinary craft. If my father were here today, he would be bragging so hard about this accomplishment while also asking, "How in the world, Ashley, did you get a cookbook?!" He was truly my biggest fan.

Thanks to the everlasting support of my family, best friends—especially my husband, Jake, and my sweet boy, Sawyer, who love and encourage me every single day. To wake up every single morning and be a mom and wife who gets to pursue her career in Hollywood is everything I ever dreamed of and more.

Big thanks to Abbe Drake, who was basically my right hand (wo)man in so many aspects of this cookbook creation, and the best producer there is! Your creative ideas and expression took this book from good to beyond. I'm so happy your magic hands contributed to this book. We are so lucky!

We appreciate you, Michael Tizzano, our editor, and everyone at Countryman Press for "taking a chance on an unknown kid" (more *Clueless* quotes). No, but really. Your support and guidance have been paramount. Lots of love to our hand-picked cookbook crew: Jen, Brett, Jesse, Lauren, and Dom. The creative magic we made together, I'll never forget. I'm so grateful for your collective talents! JP, your help in preproduction will always be appreciated! And to my sweet boo Rachelle, thanks for getting me cookbook-ready in the glam department.

And finally, this book would have never been created without the kismet union of my partner in crime, my work husband, and brother from another mother, Jimmy, who created this magical space in time where people come to escape reality, retreat back to their nostalgic places, and maybe even learn a thing or two here. This guy has been one of the most supportive, generous, and loving people in my journey, and I will never be able to express enough gratitude for the person you are and have been, Wimmy Jong! Timing is everything and I can't believe the time is now for us to have created this amazing masterpiece!

BIG HUGS to the *Feast of Fiction* family for your support for over eight years and beyond, this is for you: You are the realest ones! Okay, so this is the part where they start playing music over my acceptance speech, so I gotta go. Love y'all, bye!

Jimmy: A huge thank you to my family, who have been there supporting me in front of the camera and behind it for over eight years now in Los Angeles. My brother Freddie for helping me survive LA for years before I finally found my feet, and for helping conceptualize the original idea that eventually evolved into *Feast of Fiction*. Thanks to my mom for being an actual culinary master and for always making home-cooked meals for us growing up. You instilled a love of food and craftsmanship in me from a very young age, and for that I will forever be grateful. And to my dad for being my absolute favorite guest star on the channel, and for always making it a point to come home for dinner even as an on-call doctor, so that we could always eat as a family.

Thanks to Abbe Drake for being an incredibly talented and hardworking producer who's been with us for over five years now. Your attention to detail and ability to craft recipes, sew costumes, and produce shoots is unparalleled. We owe you so much for always elevating the quality level of our show. Andrew Manliguez and Alfred Estaca for being my ride or die brothers in business, and who have spent the long hours grinding out the work to help grow and sustain our show for so many years. Sam Waldow for masterful editing and bringing his wonderful sense of humor to each video. JP for all of the recipe preparation and testing for the cookbook prior to the shoot. Matt and Dez for being our very first support and camera crew when we first started, and everyone else who has helped behind the scenes in any way. Much love to Nancy, Petar, and the team at Addition+ who got the wheels turning on this process, and Michael and the rest of the talented staff over at Countryman Press who made this book a reality!

Thank you to our wonderful crew who made this cookbook possible! Jen Barguiarena, our incredible art director. Brett Long, our diligent food stylist. Jesse Hsu, our enthusiastic photographer. Lauren Haroutunian, our masterful director of photography (here's to seven years working together!). Dominic D'astice, master of lights and setups. Christina Wolfgram for diligently editing and making sure our essence is captured in the many lines of text throughout the book. And of course Abbe Drake and Ashley Adams, who put in endless hours testing each recipe and perfecting them for our very first cookbook. Without all these elements working together, we wouldn't be releasing this book to you today. I cannot thank everyone enough!

Finally, the biggest thanks and acknowledgment go to the one and only Ashley, who I will be forever grateful to for saying yes on that fateful day nine years ago to an idea I had in my head, and who has stuck by my side since our very first shoot, through thick and thin. I never thought we'd get to where we are today, and I'm so very grateful that you are the cohost and partner I get to cross this finish line with. Who knows what the future holds for us, but as long as you're there with me, there ain't nothing that can stop us!

Our Friends in the *Feast of Fiction* Kitchen:

Art Director: Jen Barguiarena
Food Stylist: M. Brett Long
Producer: Abbe Drake
Director of Photography: Lauren Haroutunian
Photographer: Jesse Hsu
Key Grip: Dominic D'Astice
Editorial Consultant: Christina Wolfgram
Hair & Makeup: Rachelle Blanco

Index

About the Authors

Ashley Adams is a self-taught baker and DIY expert with a passion for the '80s. A Texas native, she made the trek out West in 2010 in pursuit of her lifelong dream of becoming a TV personality. At the end of 2011, after meeting Jimmy Wong, they shot their very first episode of YouTube's *Feast of Fiction*, and have been cooking up fantasy foods together ever since. When Ashley isn't recipe testing, you can find her on the interwebs, hosting and producing a bunch of other baking- and crafting-related content. Ashley has made a handful of television appearances on Food Network, as well as cohosted a show (with Jimmy) for Food Network Digital called *The Cutting Edge*. She lives in Los Angeles with her husband, Jake, and their sweet son, Sawyer.

Jimmy Wong is a bona fide geek, actor, host, and content creator who's been making viral videos since 2010. A veteran of the Internet, his videos combine charisma, teaching, and fun into his various projects online. His videos have been viewed more than 100 million times. He starred in the live-action adaptation of Disney's *Mulan* and the hit web series *Video Game High School*, cocreated the cooking show *Feast of Fiction*, and cohosts *The Command Zone* podcast and *Game Knights* online. He lives in Los Angeles.